CAIRO PAPERS IN SOCIAL SCIENCE

VOLUME 36   NUMBER 1

Biographies of Port Said:

Everydayness of State, Dwellers, and Strangers

Mostafa Mohie

THE AMERICAN UNIVERSITY IN CAIRO PRESS

CAIRO   NEW YORK

Cover photo: Port Said: Harbor and entrance to the Suez Canal showing the building of the Suez Canal Company. The Oriental C ommercial B ureau in P ort Said.

This paperback edition first published in 2023 by
The American University in Cairo Press
113 Sharia Kasr el Aini, Cairo, Egypt
420 Lexington Avenue, Suite 1644, New York, NY 10170
www.aucpress.com

First published in an electronic edition in 2020

ISBN 978 1 649 03230 0

Library of Congress Cataloging-in-Publication Data applied for

1 2 3 4 5   27 26 25 24

Designed by Adam el-Sehemy

Contents

Contents

Acknowledgments

To the interlocutors who opened their hearts and shared their memories and experiences generously. I would not be here without you.

To Hanan Sabea, Reem Saad, Hatem Al-Rustom, Martina Reiker, Malak Rouchdy, Michael Reimer, Amr Shalakany, and Ramy Aly for the illuminating and intellectually intriguing journey.

To Alia Mossallam, who inspired me to work on Port Said.

To Adham Bakry and Mohamed Ghaly for guiding me through Port Said.

To Lina Attalah and my colleagues and friends at Mada Masr.

To Tarek Mostafa, Ayah Abu Pasha, Soha Mohsen, and Noha Fikry, thank you for helping me through this journey.

To Mozn Hassan and Omnia Khalil for always supporting me.

CHAPTER 1

Introduction

I visited Port Said twice before conducting my fieldwork between August and December 2017. The first visit was in February 2013. As a journalist, I was covering the protests after the massacre in Port Said prison.[1] I stayed for only three days, covering this intense moment, before returning to Cairo with ambivalent feelings toward the city and its people. On one hand, the city was in a rebellious mood against the police brutality; on the other, it was full of chauvinistic rhetoric about Port Said and skepticism toward the intentions of anyone from Cairo.

My second visit was illuminating for me. I returned to Port Said in January 2016 to participate in the workshop "Ihky ya tarikh," which was organized by the history scholar Alia Mossallam. I stayed for a whole week learning and discussing the different narratives about Port Said, the different approaches to reading and reconstructing history. By the end of that week, I decided that Port Said would be the topic of my research.

---

1 The massacre in Port Said prison refers to the killing of 46 of the residents of the city by police forces, during the protests that pervaded the city, objecting to the death penalties handed down against 21 defendants in the trial of the Port Said stadium massacre. The latter refers to the killing of 72 fans of the Al-Ahly football team in the riot that broke out after one of the Egyptian league matches in Port Said stadium, on 1 February 2012. The defendants in this riot were mostly Port Saidians. However, other theories about the stadium massacre suggested that it was organized by the authorities to target the Al-Ahly Ultras group because of its participation in the post-revolution protests calling for democracy and protesting police brutality. This topic will be discussed further in chapter five.

I became interested in Port Said for the following reasons. It was built as part of the project of the Suez Canal in the nineteenth century. Unlike most Egyptian cities, towns, and villages, which have a very long history that goes back thousands of years, Port Said is only 158 years old. This state of novelty affords researchers a wide range of documents, photos, maps, memoirs, and family collections, which constitutes a treasure of records of the constructions of the social since the founding of the city. The building of the city in the nineteenth century made it a field for the modernist techniques of ordering the social and the spatial, which will be explained later in this chapter. Because of the Suez Canal, the international trade, and the foreign presence in the city, mainly between 1869 and the mid 1950s, Port Said was a junction point on the global, national, and local scales, where different networks of forces define what it is as a city. With *al-'udwan al-thulathi* (the so-called Tripartite Aggression against Egypt in 1956 by the British, French, and Israeli armies), the city became a "symbol of resistance" in the nationalistic narrative. The declaration of Port Said as a free trade zone in 1975 rendered the city a symbol of the *infitah*, the economic open-door policy that started during the Sadat era. Thus the city has always represented the shifts of the Egyptian modern state, from the colonial to the national-liberation to the neoliberal eras.

It is true that Port Said is not the only city that reflects the shifts of the Egyptian modern state. Actually, every city does, because every city was affected by these shifts. However, apart from Cairo and Alexandria, the two biggest cities in Egypt, many Egyptian cities are integrated in the national narratives about the more recent history of the country. Yet the Tripartite Aggression in 1956 and the declaration of the Free Trade Zone (FTZ) in 1975 integrated Port Said into the national narratives. While the first turned Port Said into a "symbol of resistance," the second reproduced the city as an example of the *infitah* and its transformative capacity. Because of these two moments, Port Said, which is quite a small city in comparison to others in Egypt, became part of the national narratives about national liberation and the neoliberal phases of the post-colonial state. It represented these two eras and reflected the essence of these times and their major shifts.

In my research, I examined how the social of the city of Port Said has been assembled, and how the spaces of the city have been produced through the practices of its residents and the state. I focused on the processes of the making and the transformation of the people and the city in specific moments. I focused on *al-tahgir* (the forced migration of the population of the Suez Canal Zone following the outbreak of the 1967 war [*al-naksa*] between Egypt and Israel), the declaration of the Free Trade Zone in the mid 1970s and its impact on the city, which altered the trading modalities from sea trading to land trading, and the Port Said stadium massacre in 2012 and its role in the reproduction of the city.

Focusing on these moments does not mean disregarding or underestimating the importance of the other moments and phases of the city, such as the Tripartite Aggression in 1956 and the arguably "cosmopolitan" phase of Port Said, which had lasted from its founding until the 1940s. Both are major components of the narratives of the city. Both have an important role in shaping the social of the city. Although they are not discussed in this study separately in stand-alone chapters, they always exist in the background of almost every chapter, just as they always existed in the background of each interview and conversation with my interlocutors. They are not in the foreground because most of my interlocutors were born after the events took place or were too young to have strong and clear accounts about these two elements. However, the battle of Port Said in 1956 and the claimed affinity of the city with the larger world are always there, as threads, intertwined with the other elements that shape the city and the collective memory of its people.

To engage with these moments and processes of transformation, I was guided by Latour (the Actor Network Theory) and Lefebvre (the Production of Space) as the two main academic interlocutors in my research. Through the Latourian framework, I was able to see the importance of following the actors, their actions, and group formation/deformation, paying attention to the non-human actors and their contribution to the process of reassembling the social. For Latour (2005), a group cannot be studied outside the processes of its formation and deformation. There is no such group that exists by inertia; it exists only through the continuous process of excluding and including, defining its borders, and acting upon other groups. When a group is not forming itself, it ceases to exist. To study a group means to study the traces of its association, assembling, and formation. In another aspect, following actors means to "catch up with their often wild innovations in order to learn from them what the collective existence has become in their hands" (Latour 2005:8). It is an attempt to find the order in which the social is assembled by these actors, instead of imposing a certain social order. Maximizing this "actor-following plan" leads to including even non-human and immaterial actors (or actants), as long as they are able "to modify a state of affairs by making a difference" (Latour 2005:71). Further, he suggests reconsidering the sources of actions that seem non-positivist enough or do not seem scientific as sources of action that contribute to the social formation. It is not an attempt to take whatever is said by the actors as an explanation in itself, but it is an attempt to avoid imposing the researcher's metalanguage instead of listening to the metalanguage of the actors themselves. In other words, the Actor Network Theory is all about questioning the readily made classifications, categories, and explanations of the social in favor of learning more from the actors in the field, letting them guide the researcher.

Reading Lefebvre side by side with Latour emphasized the fact that space is the precondition for the social to emerge, and simultaneously it is the product of this social emergence. We cannot talk about group formations, actor movements, and objects' affects without analyzing the relationship between these and the space within which they exist and interact. For Lefebvre (1991), space cannot be theorized as a mere container of these processes and interactions. Rather, it is the precondition for the social to emerge, and simultaneously the product of this social emergence. This dialectical relationship between space and the social creates the possibility of having what Lefebvre called the social space, which "permits fresh actions to occur, while suggesting others and prohibiting yet others" (Lefebvre 1991:73). Studying spaces cannot be done merely by looking into the "things" within these spaces, or studying space as a space in itself, a mere fetishized space. Rather, it can only be understood through unpacking the social relationships that are embedded in it, and the social relationships that produced it (Lefebvre 1991:89). Lefebvre here builds on the Marxist argument against the fetishism of commodities, "where the trap lay in exchange, and the error was to consider 'things' in isolation, as things in themselves" (Lefebvre 1991:90). Further, in view of the diversity of interactions and interrelations among actors and things in any space, we are not faced here by a singular social space, but by multiple ones which do not exist juxtaposed with one another, but in relations of interlocation, combination, or superimposition (Lefebvre 1991:86).

Both theorists helped me to see the dialectical relationship between the social and space and how they reproduce each other. Just as the social is never constant—actors are merely actors because of their movements, groups are always under the condition of formation and deformation—space, in the same sense, is never constant. It is always in the making. It is always multiple, open to different meanings. That is what makes cities open-ended spaces, and always in the making. Reading Simone's (2004) work, *People as Infrastructure*, helped me to see human networks as part of the infrastructure of the cities. Through these networks, the city is transformed, and without them the city is paralyzed. De Certeau widened my understanding of the spatial practices that contribute to the production of space. With de Certeau, I started to see the acts of memorizing the past, telling stories, and singing songs as spatial practices, through which spaces are produced. Through Walter Benjamin's work, I started to understand history not as something that belongs to the past, but as something that can exist only in the present, the now-time.

Through the conversation between fieldwork and theory, I started to see the different moments that I chose to study, as moments that had destructive, yet also creative effects on the city and its people. On one hand, *al-tahgir* was an act of dismantling the social fabric of Port Said and an act of liquidating the people's networks, but on the other hand, it triggered the process of reimagining the city by Port Saidians. I chose to start this study with *al-tahgir* to highlight the heaviness and the impact of that moment on what followed, as the landmark that distinguished between what was before and what came after. *Al-tahgir*, in this narrative, is neither a moment of defeat nor a moment of resistance. Rather, it is the ultimate moment of transformation in the history of this city. The inhabitants of Port Said were evicted from the city, just as the populations of Ismailiya and Suez were evicted from the canal zone, and diffused into other Egyptian cities and villages. The action of *al-tahgir* dismantled the social fabric, and constituted a real threat to everything the Port Saidians relied on to define their existence, such as residence, working, and lifestyle. They then engaged in a process of reproducing themselves as a group, through producing the members of the host communities as the other. I argue that *al-tahgir* was one of the moments that contributed to the production of the notion of "Port-Saidness" among the residents of the city, and its opposite, *al-aghrab* (the strangers). The two notions still exist today.

Figure 1: A row of buildings overlooks the canal in Port Said. The picture was taken by G. Massaoud between 1870 and 1895.

The declaration of the Free Trade Zone in 1975 ushered in massive social and spatial transformations in the city, altering the modality of trading from sea trading to land trading. While the former was related to the maritime traffic of the canal and the foreign visitors to the city, the second was related to the local consumers who headed to Port Said to buy the imported goods that were not available in other markets in Egypt at that time. I studied the two trading modalities and how each of them produced the city and the social in different ways.

The Port Said stadium massacre had a catastrophic effect on the city, in terms of stigmatization of the Port Saidians and the economic recession after the massacre. However, it posed the question of what is Port Said, what defines it apart from the massacre, motivating various initiatives such as Port Saʻid ʻala Qadimo[2] and new *al-simsimiya*[3] bands, which contributed to the continuous processes of the making of the city. Both initiatives relied on objects that absorbed the past in themselves, such as the musical instrument *simsimiya* and the old buildings from the colonial era. Both kinds of objects have come to be nodes of interactions and relations that have contributed to the social and spatial reproduction of the city.

Port Said and the Suez Canal

This introduction presents a historical background of the construction of Port Said in the nineteenth century, explaining the way in which spaces and population were ordered.

On 25 April 1859, a group of almost 100 men, mostly Egyptian workers, and a few foreign engineers stood on a strip of land 40 to 50 meters wide between Lake al-Manzala and the Mediterranean Sea. The French diplomat and administrator of the Suez Canal project, Ferdinand de Lesseps, gave a speech and hit the land with his mattock to announce the beginning of the digging of the Suez Canal. The workers started to erect the first row of tents on the land that would be known later as Port Said (Mubarak 1886–88:26–30). The city was expanded by filling the lake with the rubble that came from the digging of the canal (Negm 1987). The inhabitants of the city were foreign and local immigrants from various countries around the world as well as various cities and villages around Egypt. They either participated directly in the digging of the Canal or came to the new city seeking new opportunities. In 1868, the population of the city was 2,700 Egyptian men and 6,000 foreigners; women, children, and older people who were not able to work were excluded from the statistics (Negm 1987:53–54). In 1882, the population reached 10,693 Egyptians and 5,867 foreigners. Greeks constituted the biggest foreign community at that time with 2,371 inhabitants. The second biggest community was the Italians, with

---

2   Port Saʻid ʻala Qadimo (Port Said as It Was) is a local initiative that works to preserve the architectural heritage of Port Said. More will be said about the initiative and its relationship with the massacre of Port Said stadium in chapter five.

3   *Simsimiya* is a popular local collective singing genre in the Canal area, which started in Port Said in the 1930s. *Simsimiya* is the name of the musical stringed instrument which is used in this genre. This topic will be explored further in chapters four and five.

1,055 people. The French numbered only 780 people, the British 775, and the Austrians 766. Other nationalities with even fewer numbers included German, Russian, Belgian, Iranian, Spanish, Dutch, and Danish (Negm 1987:55).

Multiple religious missions accompanied the increasing European worker immigrants to the Canal cities. Unlike the usual case, they were not seeking to increase their followers, but were there to support the Europeans in their religious duties and daily lives. "They not only managed places of worship, but also education and medical care" (Frémaux and Volait 2009:256). The Canal Company implemented a policy to finance and subsidize worship buildings of the various religious groups, including Muslims, who were the majority among the population of the Canal Zone. Most of this subsidization was in the form of land concessions.

This policy was meant to accommodate staff of any origin, but was also an efficient tool in the control of construction of places of worship. Every demand for subsidy required the submission of precise figures (size of community, number of Company's employees, etc.) and was to be accompanied with plans. Demands were treated favorably (and resulted in allowances or fringe benefits), once the need for a worship place had been agreed upon and after approval of the building's aesthetics had been given. (Frémaux and Volait 2009:256)

The same policy was implemented for schools, which were built on land concessions or by the Company itself (Frémaux and Volait 2009:256).

According to the franchise agreements between the Egyptian state and the Universal Maritime Suez Canal Company, the latter was mostly responsible for the urban planning of Port Said (Negm 1987). The company designed two neighborhoods, al-Ifrang (the foreigners) and al-Arab (the Arabs). At first there was empty land separating the two neighborhoods, but in time this empty land was inhabited. Al-Ifrang was built in a European style with a prestigious French architecture. Most of the hotels, department stores, casinos, restaurants, foreign banks, and other foreign companies were located in al-Ifrang. Consulates for the various foreign communities were opened, competing with Alexandria in number. The Suez Canal Company named some of al-Ifrang's streets after foreigners, such as Ferdinand de Lesseps, Empress Eugénie, Thomas Waghorn, and

François Joseph. Other streets carried the names of Ottoman and Egyptian rulers such as Sultan Murad, Sultan Othman, Sa'id Pasha, Ibrahim Pasha, and Khedive Tewfik. The neighborhood was built on the west bank of the Canal to be the façade of the city: the first thing to be seen after leaving the port, giving the spectator an impression of a European city[4] in the middle of the "oriental world."

Figure 2: A picture of King Fouad street (currently al-Gumhuriya street) in al-Ifrang neighborhood, was taken between 1925 and 1950. The photographer is anonymous but the picture belongs to the collection of the Oriental Commercial Bureau, Port Said.

The al-Arab neighborhood was built on the other side of the city, toward the west, hiding behind al-Ifrang. The Egyptians lived there in narrow wooden shacks in the early years of the city. However, after repeated outbreaks of fire in the neighborhood, the Canal Company decided to

---

4   The Port Said planners followed modernist techniques to design the city, using a grid system. James C. Scott (1998:55–59) states that planners were using grids in the nineteenth century to make cities intelligible, governable, and quantifiable, and to allow mobility, as opposed to old cities, which were unintelligible to strangers. Port Said was not the only site for these techniques in urban planning and governmentality. Timothy Mitchell explains the adaptation of modernist techniques in reconstructing Cairo in the 1860s (Mitchell 1991:63), adding that disposing people and spaces according to modern schemes was also imposed on some villages in the Nile Delta in 1846 (Mitchell 1991:44).

enforce a new building code in al-Arab, using a mix of wood and bricks to make the buildings more resistant to fire (Negm 1987:37). The streets of al-Arab were narrower than the streets of al-Ifrang, and still are. They were also named in a different way. They carried the names of the governorates and the cities from which the Egyptian immigrants came, such as Minya, al-Sharqiya, Aswan, al-Daqahliya, and Damietta. For years, the residents of al-Arab suffered from water shortages, until the Canal Company managed to construct a pipeline to supply Port Said with fresh water from Ismailiya in 1866, and to dig a freshwater canal from Ismailiya to Port Said in 1895. The company also constructed a water treatment station, using sand filters, which supplied the city with drinking water until 1906 (Negm 1987:43). However, even after solving the water issue, the Company continued to favor al-Ifrang over al-Arab. While the former neighborhood was allowed to use treated water at any time, the latter was allowed to use water only during the daytime hours (Negm 1987:43).

Figure 3: A picture of al-Arab neighborhood, taken between 1925 and 1950. The photographer is anonymous but the picture belongs to the collection of the Oriental Commercial Bureau, Port Said.

As the population of Port Said grew, more neighborhoods were built. On the eastern bank of the canal, the Canal Company built the Port Fouad district, and to the west of al-Arab, the al-Manakh neighborhood was established. The city was made up of these four neighborhoods until the 1950s. Later, the al-Dawahi (the Suburbs) district was built on the south of the city. By the end of the 1970s, al-Zuhur, which is now the most populous neighborhood, had been built and was expanding toward the west. In 1975, President Sadat issued Decree No. 651/1975 to add some of the rural villages of Ismailiya governorate to Port Said, which had previously been an urban governorate without any rural areas. Later, the al-Gharb (the West) neighborhood was added to Port Said, lying between al-Zuhur and Lake al-Manzalah, and the al-Ganub (the South) neighborhood was added to the south of the city, containing most of the agrarian land.

Stranger's Gaze

Walking through Port Said's streets reveals a lot about the city. The names of places and streets speak of its multilayered history. Differences in architecture reflect the deeply rooted divisions between the different neighborhoods. The voices of the city disclose silences in the narratives. An absence somewhere exposes a presence somewhere else. During my fieldwork, I lived in Port Fouad, on the eastern side of the Suez Canal, a few minutes from the ferry that links the two sides of Port Said. Most of my walks were in Port Said, reflecting the fact that Port Fouad is a small district compared to the other neighborhoods in Port Said. However, walking in Port Fouad reveals the many places that carry blue flags with the two characters S.C., announcing the ownership of these places by the Suez Canal Authority. The franchise agreement between Sa'id Pasha, the ruler of Egypt between 1854 and 1863, and the Canal Company secured the domination of the latter over the land of Port Said. This domination still can be seen to some extent in Port Fouad—even after the nationalization of the company in 1956—in the conspicuous residential villas for senior employees of the Canal Authority, the coastal club, the clinic, the hospital, and the school; all of them are owned by the Suez Canal Authority.

Every morning, I left my house in Port Fouad and walked to the ferry station to take one of the boats to the other side of the city. The ferry is also owned and run by the Canal Authority, and it works for free. As time passed, I started to notice that there are two different kinds of ferries. The first one consists of one level, on which cars, pedestrians, motorcycles, and bicycles all gather to cross the canal. There is a tower on the side of the ferry at the top of which is the captain's cabin. Most of these old ferries have names such as "Port Said-1" or "Sinai-2." The second kind of ferry is the "developed" ones, which are bigger and have two levels: the first level is for vehicles and the second is for pedestrians. The captain's cabin is located on the roof of the second level. On the pedestrians' level, the rows of seats are divided into three groups with three different colors: red, white, and black, the colors of the Egyptian flag. On the side of the ferry, the slogan of Abdel Fattah al-Sisi's presidential election campaign, "Long Live Egypt," is inscribed as the name of the ferry. The other side of the ferry displays the logo of "the New Suez Canal."[5] Both kinds of ferries have national slogans but from different eras. "Sinai" and "Port Said" are related to the national liberation era—wars against imperialism in 1956 and Israel in 1967–1973—while "Long Live Egypt" is related to the Sisi era when nationalism has no clear manifestations except for mega projects such as the "New Suez Canal."

Taking the ferry to Port Said replicated for me the experience of a foreign visitor who is viewing the city from outside while approaching Port Said gradually. I can see the same line of buildings on the bank of the canal. Now they are older and mostly abandoned but still intact. "Simon Arzt"—one of the oldest department stores in Port Said, built in 1923—is beside the abandoned white building of the American Consulate. The latter is close to the old lighthouse, which no longer stands in the middle of the water. Now it is surrounded by houses, after the expansion of the city into what used to be the sea. In the same line of buildings, a block of similar houses, with noticeable decorated terraces, stands on wooden beams. In one of these buildings, a spacious Indian restaurant occupies the first two floors, with a modern front that is incompatible with the rest of the building. In the same line, other tall and modern buildings exist side by side with the old ones. The ferry stops before a white building with a high tower that looks like a minaret. This building is the police station of the port. When the ferry gate is opened, pedestrians, cars, motorcycles, and bicycles mix

---

5 The "new Suez Canal" was a project that was announced by president Abdel Fattah al-Sisi in 2014 to deepen and widen the canal, allowing bigger cargo ships to travel through it. The project was introduced to the public metaphorically as the new Suez Canal.

together for a few seconds, then disperse into the side streets. Once they have left, the front yard of the police station retreats to its calm nature again. To a great extent, the disorganized movement of disembarking from the ferry resembles the movement in the city of Port Said itself. Everything is located beside its opposite, or sometimes over it, as will be explained later.

After leaving the ferry, I walk down al-Thalathini (the Thirties) Street, which cuts through the two neighborhoods of al-Ifrang and al-Arab. Al-Thalathini is not the official name of the street; it is a common nickname for Sa'd Zaghlul Street, which was de Lesseps Street originally. The nickname came from the width of the street (30 meters). Almost every street in al-Ifrang has more than one name. The first one is usually related to the colonial, Ottoman, and monarchical eras, while the second refers to one of the prominent Egyptian nationalist figures. Empress Eugénie Street became Safiya Zaghlul Street. Khedive Tewfik became Ahmad 'Urabi. Waghorn Street became Mustafa Kamel, although it is sometimes referred to as al-Tigarah (Trading) Street. Some of these streets were renamed again with names related to the national liberation era and its symbols, such as the Republic Street instead of King Fu'ad, and Shukri al-Qawatli instead of François Joseph. The neighborhood itself was renamed al-Sharq (the East).

The politics of street naming followed the changes of the powers that ruled the country. During the first decades of the city, the Canal Company named the streets of al-Ifrang after European figures who attended the canal inauguration or had strong ties to Ferdinand de Lesseps, as well as Ottoman and Egyptian rulers from Mohamed Ali's family. From the 1920s, names of nationalist figures were imposed by the state, replacing the names from the colonial/Ottoman era. From the 1950s, the names that were related to the colonial, Ottoman, and monarchical eras were wiped off the official index of the streets and replaced by national liberation symbols, such as Salah Salem, Gamal Abdel-Nasser, and Abd al-Salam 'Aref (Elgezy 2017). The antagonism between the old and new names is clear. The new names were imposed in order to decolonize the landscape of the city from the traces of the past, which is thus claimed to be wiped away. The politics of naming is a declaration from the dominant party that the past has gone, today is another day, and the old dominator is defeated. As Navaro-Yashin explains in *The Make-Believe Space*, naming places is part of the phantasmatic crafting of spaces. By using the adjective "phantasmatic," she is not suggesting that the crafting of spaces is a mere state of mind. Rather, the phantasmatic crafting functions in the materiality of the space: "[it] is part and parcel here of the materiality of this manufacture, a process of making-and-believing, or believing-and-making, at one and the same time" (Navaro-Yashin 2012:6). But as she goes on to say, changing names cannot wipe away the past. It still can be found in the objects that remained from this past.

While walking in al-Ifrang Street, I noticed the traces of the colonial architecture in the arcades of the buildings, the English and French signs of shops side by side with newer signs in Arabic, the missionary schools such as the Collège du Bon Pasteur, and the various churches of different sects such as Maronite, Armenian, and Catholic. The landscape changes completely after crossing Mohamed Ali Street (officially al-Shuhada', or Martyrs, Street), which separates al-Ifrang from al-Arab. Houses are smaller and side streets narrower in al-Arab. Some of the old buildings are still intact, built of wood with a height of two or three floors at most. However, most of them have been replaced by modern concrete buildings. Even in these new buildings, the limitations of the lot sizes are still obvious. One can find a high building standing on a very small piece of land, which makes it look like a straw of concrete. The traces of the past are also obvious in the poverty of the old wooden buildings and the small plots of land around the new concrete buildings, even though these buildings certainly cost a fortune to construct. The old grids of al-Arab still define the possibilities of the present.

Walking toward the west takes us to al-Manakh, while walking toward the south takes us to al-Dawahi. Both were almost completely rebuilt after the wars of 1956 and 1967, so the austere architecture of social housing is dominant there. Small gray concrete houses can be seen everywhere. The street names in al-Manakh also still bear the traces of the national liberation era, such as al-Gala' (Independence), al-Sha'b (People), and al-Abtal (Heroes); there is even a square that carries the name of Stalingrad (the Soviet city), signifying the relationship between Egypt and the former Soviet Union during the 1950s and 1960s. To the west of al-Manakh is al-Zuhur neighborhood. The construction of al-Zuhur started in the 1970s to absorb the population growth. The effect of what is called the "Islamic awakening" of this era can be seen here in the names of Islamic figures that were given to the blocks of houses, such as 'Omar ibn al-Khattab Block, 'Uthman ibn 'Affan Block, Bilal ibn Rabah Block, and so on. The architecture of al-Zuhur is mostly Egyptian modern, such as can be seen in new neighborhoods in Cairo: tall concrete buildings. Heading west from al-Zuhur will take us to the shore of Lake al-Manzala, which we will not be able to see because of the wall that was built on the western edge of the city, after the declaration of the Free Trade Zone, to stop smuggling across the lake. A literal shantytown, called 'Izbet Awlad 'Ouf, is squeezed between al-Zuhur and the wall.

During my fieldwork, I often moved around and met people in the Port Fouad, al-Ifrang, and al-Arab neighborhoods, where most of the material related to my topic was assembled.

Methodology and Positionality

In my fieldwork, I relied on oral history, family collections, in-depth interviews, and archival ethnography. I visited Port Said almost every week from the beginning of August to the end of December 2016. During each visit, I stayed for three to four days in the city. In the first month, I followed the snowball methodology (one interlocutor sending me to another, and so on), without forcing a specific order on my fieldwork regarding whom to meet and why, and without forcing a specific structure on my interviews. I was simply focusing on listening and building rapport, following my interlocutors. By the end of August, I started to have a map of interlocutors covering different areas in my research, while other areas of interest were still missing. Hence, I started to take the lead, asking my main interlocutors to introduce me to specific people who could cover the various areas of interest in my research where I did not yet have information. I then began to conduct semi-structured interviews with 15 interlocutors of different ages and backgrounds. Most of the time, I did not use recording machines, trying to avoid the formal setting of the interview. I met my interlocutors in the evening, making scratch notes to highlight the most important points in the interview. Afterward, I documented the interviews in my field notes. I spent the mornings wandering the city, taking notes on the different places I passed.

The variety of the interlocutors reflects the different kinds of actions I followed, such as sea trading, land trading, *al-simsimiya*, and activities related to heritage preservation. The age range of my interlocutors allowed me to cover the different historical phases of the city, from the 1950s and 1960s when sea trading was the main action in assembling the social, to the *al-tahgir* period between 1967 and 1974–1976, into the later 1970s when the Free Trade Zone opened and the trading paradigm shifted. The conversations with the younger interlocutors put more emphasis on current encounters with the city and its history, and the ongoing processes of assembling the social. Although I was aware of the importance of listening to various voices, thanks to the snowball method I had only limited access to female voices in the city, something that assuredly affected my research. It was socially unacceptable to ask for an interview with a woman from the family of an interlocutor.

I had the opportunity to access the records of the City Council, covering the period from December 1975 to August 1976, in the governorate's archive. My first intention was to read these records up through the end of the 1970s. However, my permission to access the archive was suddenly canceled by the secretary of the governor after two days, and I was "gently" asked to leave the archive office. Besides working with the official archive, I collected 12 issues of local magazines that were published in Port Said from 1976 until 1995. They provided numerous insights about the city and its transformations. Besides following these specific methods, during my stay in Port Said I tried to walk as much as my legs were able to carry me, talk to people as much as they were open to talk, and listen to the city as much as it disclosed itself.

Through the process of conducting this research my positionality shifted at different times. I was always wearing different hats during the last years of my research. Between 2005 and 2012, I was engaged to a certain extent as a political activist in different leftist groups and parties. Then I shifted totally to journalism, which turned out to be my genuine way of engagement with the political. However, while I was working in the field, I was not able to see the political in my topic. It seemed to be nothing more than an interesting social-historical study about Port Said, which is an understudied city in comparison to Cairo or Alexandria. I was thinking of my work as important only for those who want to know about Port Said, and nothing more. Later, in the last phases of writing my manuscript, I started to see how Port Said could be related to other places through the different themes that suggested themselves in this research.

For instance, studying *al-tahgir* in Port Said clarifies what kinds of processes take place after the act of displacement, what kinds of relationships evolve between the displaced people and the place they came from and the place to which they are relocated, and how they reproduce themselves in the new places. In that sense, the experience of *al-tahgir* can be related to other cases of displacement in the region, such as the Syrians during the current civil war, the evacuees from North Sinai in the last two years as part of the "war against terrorism," and even the people of the Maspero Triangle in Cairo.[6] Another example of how Port Said can be related to other places is by understanding the notion of the strangers, *al-aghrab*, the negative image of the people of the city. *Al-aghrab* is one of the themes that kept appearing in my research. It can tell us a lot about the politics of belonging and othering, which also take place in other places: what defines who belongs to the place and who does not, what constitutes a *gharib* (stranger), and why this *gharib* needs to be produced in each place. Other examples are *al-simsimiya* gatherings and Port Sa'id 'ala Qadimo walks. Both practices have the ability to generate various forms of socialization. They are more than cultural products; they are social practices that contribute to the reassembling of the social and the production of space. This can be related to other minor practices in other places that do not seem to be very influential in defining the city, but actually they are. With this new understanding of my topic and its relationship to other cases, I began to see the political in my research.

This shift in my positionality was also reflected in my voice as an author. In the first chapters of this study, the reader can hear the voice of the "disengaged" scholar, trying to understand and interpret the events he is talking about. In the last two chapters, my voice shifted to that of the "engaged scholar." This happened as a result of the new relationship with my topic that evolved during the months of fieldwork and writing. I preferred to leave this alteration of my voice in the text as evidence of how research can change the researcher. Through this journey, I have

---

6   I am referring here to the project of "developing" the Maspero Triangle district in the heart of Cairo, which led to the displacement of most of its residents. For more information, see Mohie and Ahmed 2017.

learned to look at other places through the lens of what I have learned from Port Said. During my fieldwork, I started to understand that the city is the most intimate level of practicing politics. The city is what we create and what creates us. I learned that there are two ways to read and organize cities; one is a top-down approach, and the other is the opposite. While the top-down approach creates the city as the state's or capital's project, the bottom-up approach creates the city as the people's project. By following actors, their actions, and their networks, I was trying to understand Port Said as the people's project, the people's artifact. I hope that this approach of reading cities from bottom to top will generate not only alternative knowledge about cities, but also alternative politics toward the spaces that make us and are made by us.

.

CHAPTER 2

Al-Tahgir: The Production of
the Self and the Other

When Hajj Awad started to hear the terrifying noise of the anti-aircraft guns, he realized that the Egyptian army was defeated in the war with Israel. He was 17 years old at that time. "It was obvious that the enemy was coming closer to the city, and we [the Egyptian Army] were not at the gates of Tel Aviv, as the radio was claiming," he said. The anti-aircraft guns were trying to keep the Israeli aircraft away from Port Said, securing the retreat of the Egyptian soldiers from Sinai. This was one or two days before former president Gamal Abdel Nasser gave his televised speech on 9 June 1967, admitting Egypt's defeat in the Six-Day War (*al-naksa*).[1]

For Eid, who was 35 years old in 1967, the experience was different; he needed more time to understand what happened, although he was a member of the National Guard.[2] Two weeks before the outbreak of the war, his unit was relocated to a camp in al-Qantara, a small village in

---

1 The Six Day War is also known as *al-naksa* and the 1967 war. It was fought between 5 and 10 June 1967 by Israel against Egypt (the United Arab Republic at that time), Syria, and Jordan. It ended with a massive defeat of Egypt, Syria, and Jordan. By the end of 10 June, Israel had seized the Gaza Strip (which was under Egypt administrative rule), the West Bank (which was under Jordanian administrative rule) including Jerusalem, the Sinai Peninsula, and the Golan Heights. Although Egypt regained control over Sinai later by a combination of military operations in 1973 and peace negotiations, the war changed the geopolitics of the region until the present day.

2 The National Guard is a body of paramilitary troops formed by the Egyptian state in the 1950s, as a form of civilian defense. However, they were not permanent. During the Suez Crisis and the 1967 war, people were encouraged to join the National Guard to protect their cities. For further information, see Mossallam 2012.

Ismailiya governorate, on the western side of the Suez Canal, to defend the village while the army was relocated to Sinai to stop the expected Israeli invasion from the east. The national radio was broadcasting enthusiastic speeches about the war, so long awaited, to liberate Palestine and put an end to the existence of Israel in the region, as it was rhetorically expressed at that time. Everyone was waiting for and sure about the victory. Upon the outbreak of the war and the incursion of the Israeli army into Sinai, the radio kept the same tone, talking about imaginary victories of the Egyptian army over the Israelis, until the moment when the Israeli shells started to hit al-Qantara.

Chaos ensued, and people started to flee the village. After the train station was destroyed, people went to Port Said by truck and crossed Lake al-Manzala by boat to reach Damietta, as it was witnessed by Eid. "We were confused in the camp . . . we did not even see an enemy to fight," he said. They were under the fire of Israeli cannons and aircraft with neither officers nor clear instructions to inform them about what to do. "My colleagues in the camp started to flee," he went on. With other civilians, he jumped into a truck that was heading to al-Sharqiya, one of the Nile Delta governorates, where he and other soldiers were summoned by the military police and taken to Cairo in military trucks. "We had no idea where they were taking us. We did not realize what had happened; we neither understood nor believed it." Eid continued to describe the shock: "When we arrived in Cairo, the streets were blocked by people who were protesting Abdel Nasser's resignation, asking him to remain in office; that was the moment when we realized that we were defeated." It was already 9 June when Nasser admitted the defeat and announced his decision to step down. The following day, he revoked his resignation, after the massive protests in Cairo asking him to stay.

Eid spent the night in a military camp in Cairo before he was taken back to al-Qantara. He stayed there for two nights, then he was sent to Port Said for another two nights. Later he was relocated to Port Fouad, where he remained for a week in a soldiers' trench. After that, he was dismissed, his unit in the National Guard was dissolved, and he went back to Port Said.

Despite the fact that the destruction in Port Said was less than in Suez and Ismailiya, many families left the city after the outbreak of the war. After several weeks, when the cease-fire came into effect, some of these families returned to Port Said. Radwan, who was ten years old at that time, described this migration wave as the "small migration" (*al-higrah al-sughra*), to distinguish it from the "great migration" (*al-higrah al-kubra*) in 1969, when the state imposed its decision to relocate the population of the Canal Zone to other cities in Egypt until the end of the war. *Al-higrah al-sughra* was unorganized, spontaneous, and lasted for a short time. It is true that some families left Port Said and did not come back until the end of the war in 1973. However, the majority of the families returned after a few weeks, especially those who worked for government offices and institutions, such as Radwan's parents, who worked in the telecommunications station. Radwan's family stayed for a few weeks in the city of Shirbeen, in al-Daqahliya governorate in the Nile Delta, where Radwan's uncle lived. Then they returned to Port Said, mainly because of work and the beginning of the school year in September.

It was easier for families from the upper classes to flee Port Said with valuable belongings that enabled them to start new lives in other cities. Also, families with strong ties to their relatives in their hometowns and villages were able to migrate to these hometowns and stay there. On the other hand, families who had been established in Port Said for two or three generations were not able to do the same; ties with the relatives in hometowns and villages had weakened with time, which made it difficult for them to find a way to escape. These families stayed in Port Said waiting for the unknown. Hajj Awad gave an account of this period. His family members were mainly tradesmen. Although they went through a tough time after their business closed, they were not able to leave Port Said. "We didn't have any place to go," he explained. Hajj Awad was born in Port Said in 1950; his father arrived in the city as a child, with his father. Hajj Awad belongs to the third generation of an immigrant family, just like other families in Port Said that migrated to the city after its construction.

After the 1967 war, time passed slowly and heavily in the city as if it were frozen. "Life stood still. The traffic in the canal stopped. All of the activities related to ship traffic stopped, trade, tourism, ship services, and so on," Hajj Awad emphasized. He answered my question about how they lived during those days by saying, "We barely managed our lives. If we did not have enough money to buy food one day, one of us would go fishing to feed the family. Whoever had money was lending to whoever did not have it. And life went on in that way." Yet despite the deep impact of the war, Port Said was not fully dead. According to Radwan, some institutions and activities continued to function, such as schools, hospitals, services, and internal trade. The ferry kept its daily schedule, crossing the Suez Canal and linking between Port Said and Port Fouad. On the other hand, the military occupied both peripheral and central spots in the city. There was a military camp close to al-Gamil Airport in the northwest of Port Said and another one in the Golf area in the southeast of the city. Anti-aircraft artilleries were located on top of some buildings in strategic spots in Port Said. Life continued in this way for almost two years, until the moment of the great migration, *al-higrah al-kubra*, arrived.

With the intensification of the *harb al-istinzaf* (the "war of attrition"), the state decided to evacuate the Suez Canal Zone. This act of evacuation was referred to as *al-tahgir* (the forced migration). Nearly one million people were displaced from the three governorates, Port Said, Ismailiya, and Suez, and relocated to different cities and villages around Egypt. The population of the three cities was 810,700, out of the national population of 36,626,204, at that time. Port Said was inhabited by 262,270 people, while the population of Ismailiya was 353,975, and the population of Suez was 193,965 (Abdel Shakur, Mehanna, and Hopkins 2005:25). For the Port Saidians, the process of *al-tahgir* took place between April and June 1969. For the population of Suez and Ismailiya, it started in September 1967 (Abdel Shakur, Mehanna, and Hopkins 2005:25–26). Most of the Port Saidian evacuees were pushed toward the Nile Delta governorates of al-Daqahliya and Damietta, while the people of Suez were relocated to the two governorates of Suhag and Qena in Upper Egypt, and the people of Ismailiya were relocated to al-Sharqiya and Qena (Abdel Shakur, Mehanna, and Hopkins 2005:25–26). The government managed to keep most of the evacuees (*al-muhaggarin*) away from Cairo, which was already considered overcrowded with its 4 million population at that time (Abdel Shakur, Mehanna, and Hopkins 2005:27). However, some of the upper- and middle-class population of the three cities managed to get into Cairo and Alexandria (Abdel Shakur, Mehanna, and Hopkins 2005: 27).

After the outbreak of war again in 1973, the Egyptian military was able to regain control over the east bank of the Suez Canal, and the

Egyptian government started the long process of negotiations with the Israeli government, which ended in a peace treaty in 1979. However, the population of the Suez Canal Zone was allowed to return to their homes, beginning on 31 December 1974, according to the record of the local council of Port Said. As I was told by most of my interlocutors, the people continued to return until 1976.

Yet at the moment of the forced migration out of Port Said, no one could anticipate that they would come back to their homes again in less than a decade. The state played a major role in organizing the migration, despite the fact that some families relied on their personal links to find shelter. In general, the Ministry of Social Affairs was responsible for administering the migration, side by side with the Arab Socialist Union, which was the country's sole political party at that time. The migration of those who worked for government institutions was handled by their institutions, to ensure that the employees obtained jobs equivalent to what they did in Port Said. The various state bodies collaborated to carry out the processes of assembling people, conveying them to their hosting cities and villages, finding temporary shelters, arranging for schooling, retaining jobs for those who were working for the government, and managing the problems between the evacuees and the hosting communities.

On the migration day, the people were asked to gather in specific spots in their neighborhoods. Hajj Awad and his family, with their neighbors, were directed to an empty area near the police station in al-Manakh, while others from al-Arab assembled in Sa'd Zaghlul Park, which is close to the al-Arab police station. Most of *al-muhaggarin* were allowed to take with them only their clothes and light valuables. The civil servants took them to buses and loaded their belongings into trucks. "We had no idea where we were being taken to until we arrived in Biyala city in Kafr al-Sheikh governorate," Hajj Awad remembered. His family was resettled in a public school that had been prepared as a shelter. "We were three families in one classroom, separated by curtains," he said. Schools, football fields, and rural guest houses (*mandarah*) were set up as shelters for *al-muhaggarin*. Students were assigned to other schools, and government employees had jobs equivalent to what they did in Port Said, while self-employed persons received monthly allowances from the Ministry of Social Affairs, in proportion to the number of family members.

During *al-tahgir*, many families managed to find better places to stay. Indeed, most of my interlocutors who went through the experience of *al-tahgir* moved at least twice during that time. Some families, who had been distributed among different cities, tried to reunite by moving. These family separations happened mainly because of the different migration plans that were enacted by different institutions. For instance, if the father of a family was self-employed, and his son was an employee of the Suez Canal Authority, the former might be relocated to one of the Nile Delta villages, while the latter might go to Alexandria. Those who were government employees were following the migration plan of their respective institutions, while the self-employed were following the plan of the Minister of Social Affairs. Further, because of the differences between the rural host places and the urban city of Port Said, most of the self-employed individuals were not able to carry on the same work they had done in Port Said. They had to adjust to the situation by changing either their work or their location. Hajj Awad worked in construction, although he had worked in trading in Port Said. He lived in Biyala city in Kafr al-Sheikh with his sister and mother for several months. Later, they moved again to Alexandria to reunite with his brother, who had managed to rent an apartment there. Radwan emigrated with his family to Shirbeen. Radwan's father worked for half of each month for an oil company in Alexandria, and the other half in Port Said. He was one of the *mustabqayin*, who were kept by the government in the Canal cities to run necessary services for the military, such as power and water stations, hospitals, and telecommunications. After a year of moving among three different cities, the father managed to find an apartment for the family in Damietta, less than an hour's drive from Port Said, which made it easier for him to stay in contact with his family. Another interlocutor, Hamza, was separated from his family during the migration in 1969. He was 23 years old at that time. He was forcibly migrated to Zefta city in al-Gharbiya governorate, while his family was located to al-Munufiya. Later, he moved to Talkha city in al-Daqahliya and rented an apartment, and his family joined him there.

Despite the temporariness of *al-tahgir*, which lasted for five to seven years, it had a deep impact on the evacuees. The process reproduced the Port Saidians as "evacuees" (*muhaggarin*); a new subjectivity was crafted through the documents and practices of both the state and the individuals.

Although this subjectivity was expected to be temporary, it lasted even after returning to Port Said. Starting from the 1970s onward, the figure of *al-muhaggar* (the singular of *al-muhaggarin*) has become part and parcel of people's claims to the city, identifying who deserved access to the city and its services. In addition, the Port Saidian people engaged in a complex process of remaking the self by producing an "other," namely the host communities. A discursive process of making the city and its residents began during the migration period, based on the "distinctiveness" of both Port Said and the Port Saidians. In my interviews that discussed the migration period, most of my interlocutors highlighted their perceptions of the distinction between the Port Saidians and the others, drawing a borderline between the urban area from which they came and the rural areas to which they emigrated; the "modern and civilized" appearance of the Port Saidians and the "primitiveness" of the host communities; the "openness" of Port Said to the world and the "parochial" character of the rural areas. My interlocutors regarded all of these characteristics as forming the "uniqueness" of Port Said. In the following sections of this chapter, I attempt to unpack these processes to emphasize how they contributed to the making of the social of Port Said.

Forced Migration as a Moment of Rupture

In this chapter, I build on the literature about forced migration from the Suez Canal Zone after the 1967 war (Abdel Shakur, Mehanna, and Hopkins 2005), and the old Nubian villages in 1964 (Mossallam 2012; Fernea and Kennedy 1966). Both were relevant for me to understand the impact of the forced migration on the social of the Port Saidians during and after *al-tahgir*. Further, to conceptualize the processes of producing the narratives about the Port Saidians and Port Said during the years of forced migration, I relied on the work of Khalili (2007) on the mnemonic narratives in the Palestinian refugee camps in Lebanon, and the reflections of Das (2007) on the eventual and the ordinary in the lives of the Indian people after the violent events in 1947 and 1984.

In their work on the forced migration from the Suez Canal Zone after the 1967 war, Abdel Shakur, Mehanna, and Hopkins draw on personal testimonies, not to reconstruct the history but to construct "a composite picture of personal pasts" (2005:24), reflecting contemporary values. Fernea and Kennedy's work on forced migration from Old

Nubia focused more on the transformations of the social and economic life after the migration, and the coping mechanisms that developed in the first year after the migration, which was useful for me in studying the coping mechanisms of the Port Saidians during the migration years. Mossallam (2012) focused more on the altered narratives that evolved before, during, and after the migration, and the justification for the different positions taken during these periods. In my work, I focused on the narratives that were formed and developed during and after *al-tahgir* and their effects on the production of the self and the city.

Khalili's (2007) work in the Palestinian refugee camps in Lebanon focuses on the mnemonic practices not as psychological or cognitive acts of remembering but as social practices that construct and are constructed by the social and political contexts that mutually shape the individual and collective memories. She argues that the mnemonic practices worked as containers for specific narratives, constituting significant facets of the refugees' identity and different ways to understand their past. In that sense, I argue that the past is not constant, and memories were not merely shaped in the past. Recalling the past is always a process that belongs to the now-time, as emphasized by Benjamin (1969a). Past and present mutually constitute each other. In her work, Khalili follows the transformation in mnemonic narratives from heroic to tragic. The former emerged "when the predominant local institutions are political factions that use the rich Third-Worldist transnational discourse of national liberation to appeal and mobilize a local audience of Palestinians and move them to militant activism" (Khalili 2007:734), while the latter were forged during Lebanon's post–civil war era, when NGOs replaced the political parties (Khalili 2007:734). In this chapter, I explore how the mnemonic practices of the Port Saidians produced a specific narrative about themselves during and after the *al-tahgir* years.

To theorize *al-tahgir* as a moment of rupture in the city and the lives of its residents, I relied also on Veena Das's work. In her book *Life and Words: Violence and the Descent into the Ordinary*, Das (2007) reflects on her studies of two violent moments: the partitioning of India in 1947, and the assassination of the then–prime minister Indira Gandhi in 1984. She poses questions about the relationship between these two violent moments as critical events, and everyday life before and after these events. Along with her intellectual journey, she attempts to answer the question "What happens to the subject and the world when the memory of such events is folded into the ongoing relationships?" (Das 2007:8). I will answer the question with her words:

> *My engagement with the survivors of riots also showed me that life was recovered not through some grand gestures in the realm of the transcendent but through the descent into the ordinary. There was, I argue, a mutual absorption of the violent and the ordinary so that I end up by thinking of the event as always attached to the ordinary as if there were tentacles that reach out from the everyday and anchor the event to it in some specific ways.* (Das 2007:7)

In this chapter, I attempt to follow the mutual absorption of ordinary life before *al-tahgir* and later life during the years of the forced migration of the Port Saidians.

Making the Self

During *al-tahgir*, uprooting the Port Saidians from their city and relocating them to strange environments launched a process of making the self through producing the other. In the moment of *al-tahgir* from Port Said, no one knew when they would be allowed to return. As a result, the Port Saidians started to reinvent their hometown, through practices, beliefs, and songs. However, by using the term "reinventing" I do not suggest that this process of making the self was merely an imaginary process that took place in the emigrants' minds. On the contrary, I argue that it was a process that relied on the materiality of their lives in their city before the war, and was reflected in their perception of their experience during *al-tahgir*.

When I asked Radwan about his experience with the host communities during *al-tahgir*, he told me "there was admiration for the Port Saidians. We used to deal with the host communities in a civil and urbane manner." Radwan was in Shirbeen. However, he attributed to the Port Saidians the introduction of the very basic idea of "money" in commercial transactions to the people of Shirbeen. "The barber was bartering two eggs for a haircut. When we came to the city, we were paying two piasters for the hairdresser. Then the barber started to grumble about the locals who kept giving him eggs," Radwan said, laughing.

Although it is still hard to believe that the population of a city in the Nile Delta was still bartering until the late 1960s, the same idea was repeated in different interviews. When I asked Hajj Awad why he did not keep his original profession as a tradesman during *al-tahgir* instead of working on construction, he replied in a sarcastic tone, "Our trading is different from their trading. They [the locals] were selling eggs." Before *al-tahgir*, Hajj Awad used to work in a souvenir shop owned by his family, selling imported clothes, leather goods, oriental souvenirs, and the like. Their clients were mainly foreign tourists and sailors who were crossing the canal, as well as Egyptian visitors—mostly from Cairo—during the summers. "[The locals'] lives were different from ours. They used to manage their lives with what they had in their hands. But we used to enjoy the day, to eat three meals every day. They were eating whatever was available in their houses. We used to buy what we needed," Hajj Awad explained.

Hamza also emphasized the idea that the locals were not used to buying all their needs from the market. Instead, they produced basic items such as food and clothes at home. During his stay in Zefta, he would buy frozen fish from Damietta and Mansura and sell them in Zefta to earn his living, while his father in al-Munufiya had no opportunity to trade with the locals because of their self-sufficient households. Radwan also brought up another point: the people of Shirbeen did not rent out their houses. During *al-higrah al-sughra*, Radwan's family had a hard time finding someone who would lease them an apartment. "My uncle walked the whole city to find someone who would agree to lease us a house, and he hardly could, although there were vacant apartments. The people of Shirbeen built their houses for their families, sons, and daughters. It was shameful for them to let a stranger live in their houses." Later, during *al-higrah al-kubra*, more people in Shirbeen started to accept the idea of leasing their houses.

Radwan portrayed the "cultural superiority" of the Port Saidians over the locals in other ways as well. "I was a star in the school of Shirbeen, although I was an average student in Port Said. The most insignificant student from Port Said was better than the most outstanding student in Shirbeen." He justified his argument by clarifying that he was enrolled in a private school in Port Said, and this was the reason why he mastered English and French, while the students of the public schools in

Shirbeen were just beginning to learn foreign languages. Radwan attributed a lot of the "Port Saidian supremacy" to the effect of the foreigners on the city and its Egyptian residents. "The Port Saidian teachers were better than the locals. They improved the education in Shirbeen schools during *al-tahgir*. The same could be said about the other professions and crafts," Radwan added.

This skillfulness was attributed to the knowledge that was transmitted from the foreigners in Port Said to the Egyptians. In addition, the competition between the two groups in the local labor market in Port Said enforced a high level of skillfulness among Egyptian professionals and artisans. Before *al-tahgir*, Eid was a carpenter in one of the workshops in Port Said that was owned by an Egyptian. Later, he joined the Suez Canal Authority after it was nationalized by the Egyptian state. He illustrated a schema of the existence of the foreigners in the labor market of Port Said: "The Italians and Greeks were skillful artisans, while the French people were working mainly in the administrative work in the Suez Canal Company." For him, it was important for the Egyptian workers to be skillful enough to compete with the Italians and Greeks. And, he said proudly, "truly, we were skillful." The Western clothing favored by Port Saidians was also attributed to the foreigners' existence in the city. Eid remembered with a smile that, in Port Said during his childhood in the 1940s and 1950s, "wearing a *galabiya* meant that you were still new to the city, a newcomer. Most of the Port Saidians were dressed like the foreigners [the Westerners]. You could be penniless but you took care of your clothes. During *al-tahgir*, the Port Saidian was recognized by how he looked," referring to the Western clothing of the Port Saidians in contrast to the local clothing of the members of the host communities, who were wearing the *galabiya*.

It is clear from these accounts that the interlocutors remembered themselves as actors who affected the host communities. They attributed to themselves many changes in the local culture and consumption behavior of the host communities. This emphasis on the ability of the Port Saidians to affect others was an attempt to invert the passive image of the displaced person. Most of the interlocutors used plural nouns when talking about their experience during *al-tahgir*. They talk about the experience of the "Port Saidians" as a group: how they were recognized, how they affected the host communities, and so on.

Drawing on Latour (2005), this plurality intends to create a collective sense of the Port Saidians; it is a group-formation act upon the other groups, the host communities. Linking this to Khalili's (2007) work on mnemonic narratives, this is how the collective identity of the Port Saidians—as urbanized, developed, and open to the world—was reinvented during *al-tahgir*, through sharing these stories about themselves as a group. *Simsimiya* gatherings similarly played a major role in forging the collective identity of the Port Saidians. During *al-tahgir*, they sang to Port Said, sustaining their hope that one day *al-muhaggarin* would return to their city. These gatherings worked as ritualistic practices, through which a collective identity was formed and group formation took place.[3]

Their feeling of alienation from their home pushed the Port Saidians not to be absorbed into the host communities. Radwan emphasized that the Port Saidian community was strongly interconnected during *al-tahgir*. There was a sense of understanding and empathy among them, based on sharing the same culture. "The Port Saidian was looking for a fellow Port Saidian to live close to him," he explained. In Damietta, Radwan and his family lived in the Ard al-'Asar area. "Eighty percent of the buildings in this place were inhabited by Port Saidians. Landlords even built new apartments for us, especially since most of the Port Saidians in this area were from the middle class who could afford to pay their rents," he said.

Many marriages between Port Saidian families were arranged during *al-tahgir* because of this communal sense. It was usual for Port Saidians to intermarry instead of marrying from the host communities, to avoid problems that might arise from the cultural differences, and to secure the possibility of returning to the city after the end of the war. "People were afraid that a husband or a wife from the host community would refuse to go to Port Said after the end of the war," Radwan explained. Another interlocutor, Ghali, told me that his father was very eager to register his children, who were born during *al-tahgir*, as Port Saidians, rather than according to where they were born. However, Ghali's family did not return to Port Said until 1976. During that period, the father visited the city repeatedly, accompanied by his son, who was ten years old at that time. Ghali's first memories

---

3 *Simsimiya* will be discussed further in chapter four.

of the city were forged in these visits. He still remembers how the city was destroyed after the war. The scene of the horizon full of the shacks of returnees who lost their houses in the war still haunts his mind.

The conditions of *al-tahgir* generally created a strong attachment to Port Said. For instance, Hamza did not stop visiting Port Said during this time, although it was risky as the war of attrition intensified. He managed to obtain permits from the military intelligence to visit the city, which had been turned into a military zone. He would stay there for a couple of weeks and then return to the Nile Delta. When I asked him what he was doing in Port Said during his visits, he replied, "I was visiting my family house in the al-Arab neighborhood, making sure that it was still intact. During the weeks of my stay in Port Said, I used to work for a fish restaurant close to my house." Hamza still lives in the same house, and he now runs his own small fish restaurant with his son. During these visits, he witnessed the mass destruction. The scenes are still vivid in his mind. He told me that in one of the raids a man was running down the street, trying to seek a shelter. A bomb fell close to him. The explosion did not kill the man directly but a fragment from the bomb beheaded him. The man's body kept moving for several steps before falling down on the ground. After each raid, Hamza joined others in collecting the corpses from the ruined buildings to bury them together in the martyrs' tomb, in the city's cemetery, without either headstones or religious rituals.

Despite these terrifying scenes, Hamza kept visiting the city during the war, not only to check his family's belongings but also to ensure something more. Hamza's visits to the city during the war were more like an attempt to reconnect with the life he used to have in Port Said before *al-tahgir*. It was an attempt to revisit this life, even if it did not look the same. Staying at the same house and doing the same work produced a sense of familiarity, ensuring that his existence, as he used to identify it, did not vanish. What Hamza visited was the rubble of his past life. The war and *al-tahgir* had transformed this life into rubble, yet he was able to recognize the traces of his destroyed life in the debris of the city, but not in Zefta. Or, as it was described by de Certeau (1984:108), "There is no place that is not haunted by many different spirits hidden there in silence, spirits one can 'invoke' or not. Haunted places are the only ones people can live in."

People used to identify their existence through various practices and modes of existence, such as their dwelling, their work, and their lifestyle. Space, which enables these practices and is also constructed by these practices, becomes part of this existence. For the Port Saidians, *al-tahgir* represented a threat to the practices and modes of existence with which they identified. During *al-tahgir*, the Port Saidians lost the thing that materially defined their existence, the city. As a reaction, they immersed themselves in an extensive effort to reinvent this home city. This reinvention process took the shape of reproducing the self through portraying the other (the host communities) as rural, primitive, and parochial, although Zefta, Biyala, and Shirbeen—all of which served as host cities—were not villages but cities. Yet, for my interlocutors, none of these cities was enough for them, because none of them was Port Said. The self-reliant households and the non-Western clothes were perceived as signs of primitiveness; although they are not primitive by their nature, they were produced as such. The binary was emphasized to remake the self through othering the other. By making this distinction, my interlocutors were able to identify themselves again, protecting the existence that was threatened by *al-tahgir*. Zefta, Biyala, and Shirbeen had to be produced as primitive places to reproduce Port Said as the urban and civilized hometown.

A similar process of reinventing the homeland as "blessed" took place in the case of the Nubian migrants. Fernea and Kennedy (1966:349) state that most of the Nubians "considered the climate, land, and water superior to that found anywhere else in the Nile valley, and they believed their villages, which were relatively free of outside interference, to have the highest standards of peacefulness, cleanliness, honesty, and personal security in Egypt," although they were aware of the social and economic disadvantages of their old and isolated villages. Mossallam (2012) explains this ambivalence further by highlighting the forms of estrangements Nubians experienced in the new villages to which they relocated: their distance from the Nile, the differences between the traditional Nubian houses and the new ones, the poor quality of the agricultural land in the new villages, and the lack of security that comes with living among Upper Egyptians and "fellahin," as they called them. For them, the new villages remained *bilad al-tahgir* (the "migration land"), as if migration "is something that is still happening; thus the process never ended, and on the contrary is being kept alive" (Mossallam 2012:183).

Although *al-muhaggarin* remained inside Egypt and were not pushed outside the country, they felt like strangers in the hosting cities and villages. It is true that most of my interlocutors acknowledged that they were mostly treated well by the host communities. However, the cultural differences, and the threat to their existence as they perceived it, increased their feeling of vulnerability. It is astonishing how this sense of vulnerability was mixed with claims of cultural supremacy. The relationship between the two is not one of coexistence. Rather, it is co-constitutive. Ordinary life before the war was mobilized during *al-tahgir* to produce these claims of cultural supremacy, in the same way that Das (2007) compares the eventual and the ordinary. But the question is how the eventual was absorbed in the ordinary, what remained of *al-tahgir*, and how this was reflected in the aftermath.

Producing *al-Aghrab*

One day in October 2016, I visited the social solidarity office in Port Said, trying to find any records about *al-tahgir*, such as the number of displaced people, statistics about the distribution plan of *al-muhaggarin*, and the like. Radwan had told me that I might find this kind of record there. The Ministry of Social Affairs (currently the Ministry of Social Solidarity) was one of the government bodies responsible for managing *al-tahgir* from Port Said, as I was informed by different interlocutors. Radwan, who occupied a senior position in the governorate administration of Port Said, managed to guide me through the bureaucratic maze. He accompanied me to the social solidarity office and introduced me to the female employee who was responsible for the information center in the office. I explained what I was doing and what I needed. However, she said that they had nothing of what I was asking for. "We don't have any records or statistics related to *al-tahgir*. We merely have the migration cards, *kroot al-tahgir*," she replied. I asked her what she meant by the migration cards. She replied, "These cards were produced during *al-tahgir*, where the information of every *muhaggar* is recorded."

Although I was disappointed by this information, I asked the employee to show me the cards. I expected to move to an abandoned room, covered with dust and full of files that had no use except as a good meal for rats. Contrary to my imagination, I just stepped outside the office and moved two steps toward another room on the same floor. The room did not seem abandoned at all; it was inhabited by four employees, two men and two women, sitting by two desks, about to have their breakfast. The opposite wall was half covered by bluish-gray drawers that contained the migration cards in alphabetical order. One of the female employees started to explain, "In this room, we have only the cards of *al-muhaggarin* who were self-employed. The Ministry of Social Affairs was responsible for managing the migration of this group, while those who worked for government institutions were the responsibility of their institutions and offices." Then she went on, "We keep the cards for the times when people ask for them." And that was a surprise; why does anyone still need to ask for these cards?

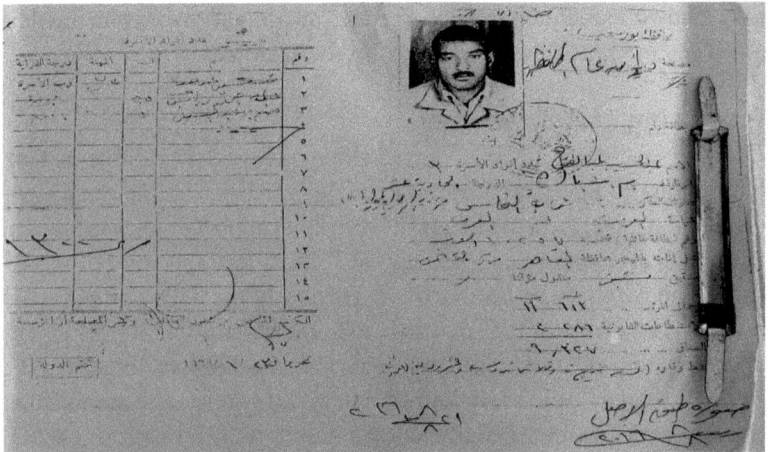

Figure 4: A photocopy of a migration document of a public servant. On the back of the document, it is mentioned that he is not eligible for the monthly allowance.

During *al-tahgir*, migration documents, *watha'iq al-tahgir*, were produced by the government and delivered to *al-muhaggarin*. These documents were used to facilitate receiving monthly allowances, registering students in school, opening businesses, exempting from public transport fees, and so on. In general, they were used to govern *al-muhaggarin* and to administer the relocation process. The *wathiqat al-tahgir* (migration document) did not merely create the status of *al-muhaggar*, it transformed the evacuee into a legal subject. The emigrant's state of migration became a legal matter, which could be proven and contested.

However, I did not expect to find all of these dynamics still in effect. I asked the employee, "Why does anyone still need to ask for these cards?" and she answered,

> *When anyone wants to get one of the social housing apartments in the city, the person needs to present a proof that he or she is from Port Said. Then the person comes to us and we search for the card of their fathers or grandfathers [the person who was part of the migration plan]. Then we issue a certificate to say that the ancestor of this person was part of the government's migration plan.*

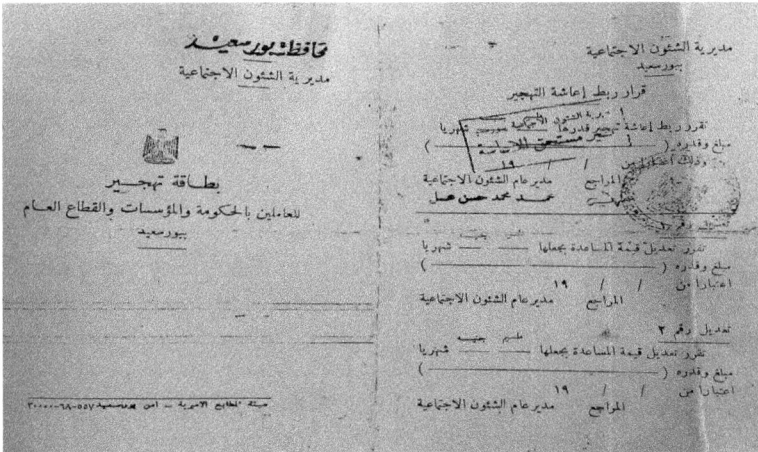

Figure 5: The back of the migration document, which mentions the name of the migrant, his job, address, salary, and his family members' names.

According to what I was told by the employee, the migration cards were used as proof of "indigeneity," supporting the person's claim to residence in the city. I asked the employee why they needed to rely on migration cards instead of national IDs or birth certificates to ensure the "Port Saidian legal identity" of the person. The answer was that documents like national IDs and birth certificates identify the current status of the person but not the status of "origin." A person might be born in Port Said but the parents could be from another city, or the person might live in Port Said but he or she is a newcomer to the city. So they choose to consult the migration cards. For those who were working for government institutions, their descendants can have certificates from the same institutions that their family member worked for. Those who migrated on their own can request a certificate of their family record from the civil registry office to prove that they are from Port Said.[4]

All of these documents deal with the moment of *al-tahgir* as the reference point that determines who is a Port Saidian and who is not, and as a result, who has the right to the city and its services and who does not. When these cards were first produced, they were not intended to be used in this manner. However, they have become one of the foundations that define who is a real Port Saidian, and to distinguish between locals and newcomers, especially during the reconstruction of the city after 1974. The moment of the migration was the perfect moment to be used as a reference point to define "Port-Saidness" as a legal identity. The state managed to evict almost all of the population of the city, except those who had to remain (*al-mustabqayin*); these people were also issued special documents. During this process, family members were counted and their names, ages, and jobs were recorded in the migration cards (the copy the government kept) and the migration documents (the copy the families kept). The documents, initially produced as a governing tool during migration, were reused later as proof of being Port Saidian.

In that sense, the migration documents became actors according to the Latourian framework. They are actors as long as they are able "to modify a state of affairs by making a difference" (Latour 2005:71). Indeed, they played a major role in defining who has the right to the city and who does not, who is a real Port Saidian and who is not. The migration documents thus played a role as an actor in forming the Port Saidians as a group. It can be said that, just as the migration document produced the legal status of the migrant, it affirmed the legal status of the Port Saidian after the return to the city. In other words, the legality of the migrant was transmitted to the returnee and was used to produce the Port Saidian as a legal subject. And, like any legal claim, it can be proven or contested.

---

4   It should be mentioned here that additional regulations were added to facilitate the process of having access to the city services. At present, it is not solely the migration documents that prove the "indigenousness" of a person. One can also support one's claim by providing proof of ten years of continuous work or residency in the city to apply for a social housing apartment, receive a tax-free car licence, or acquire an "import permit" to work in the Free Trade Zone.

Proof of Port-Saidness is always a matter of contestation in Port Said. It is almost impossible to have a conversation with a Port Saidian without mentioning the strangers, *al-aghrab*, and their negative impact on the city, which is astonishing in a city that was constituted in the first place by strangers from all over Egypt. The questions of when this Port-Saidness identity is gained and why it is so important are difficult to answer fully. I am not suggesting that the Port Saidian identity was created by the migration documents. Rather, I argue that the migration document, like any state document, created the legality of the evacuee, the returnee, and the Port Saidian, producing a sort of legitimacy for their claims to the city. Conversely, the document deprived others of this legitimacy: the strangers, *al-aghrab*.

To understand the context of the production of the legality of the Port Saidian and the illegitimacy of the stranger, I will quote Radwan, who gives an account of the moment of the return to the city after 1974.

The moment of return was the hardest. The people from the middle class started to return to the city immediately after the war. A lot of buildings were totally destroyed or needed repair. Most of the destruction happened during the 1973 war,[5] and not like Suez and Ismailiya, which were destroyed during the 1967 war. At the end, the level of destruction that happened in Port Said during the 1973 war was similar to what happened to the other Canal cities. There were a lot of victims among al-mustabqayin. *When the people started to return, they did not know if their houses were still there or not, especially those who had no* mustabqayin *among their relatives to tell them about their houses. People were carrying their belongings and going to the city. Some of them arrived in Port Said to find that their houses were destroyed; they stood before their ruined houses with no idea what to do. Most people lost their savings during* al-tahgir. *Others lost their houses because they simply stopped paying the rent when they were away from the city. During* al-tahgir, *people did not know when they*

---

5 Many of my interlocutors attributed the lesser destruction of Port Said to the fact that it was protected by the existence of Port Fouad on the other side of the Canal. Port Fouad was the only spot in the Sinai peninsula that was not occupied by Israel (Hassan 2016). However, with the intensification of the war of attrition, Port Said was targeted by more raids and by the end of the 1973 war the destruction of the city was almost similar to Suez and Ismailiya.

*would be able to return to their lives, or even if that would happen at
any moment soon. The image of the Palestinian refugees was vividly
present in their minds.*[6] *Others lost their houses because the landlord
wanted to write new contracts with higher rents. Generally, there
was a massive social mobilization toward the bottom. The service sector in the city was paralyzed. The merchants had no capital to start
with; the buyers had no money to buy. It was an economic vacuum.
Some people had to live in shacks, waiting for resettlement by the government. The state started to prepare temporary shelters in schools for
those who lost their houses. The shelters were not only for poor people
but also for middle-class families who lost their houses; among them,
there were others who came to the city and claimed to be Port Saidians
[to take advantage of the resettlement].*

Radwan's account raised my curiosity about the category of *al-
aghrab*, who were mostly depicted as "opportunity seekers" when they
were mentioned in my interviews. I suggest that this narrative of *al-
aghrab* was intensified after the moment of the return to the city and
lasted for a long time, as will be discussed later in this chapter. *The New
Port Said* was a monthly local magazine that began to be published in
the early 1980s. In the April 1983 issue, an opinion column by Qasim

6   In the same interview, Radwan suggested that the government intended to use the
word *muhaggarin* (migrants) instead of "refugees" to avoid any reference to the
Palestinian refugees. Also, one interpretation of the government's decision to distribute
migrants around Egypt instead of building refugee camps was to escape the parallel to
the Palestinian refugees. However, I think this decision was made to take advantage of
the capacity of the major cities to absorb the stream of migrants. In general, it can be
said that the government and the people had the Palestinian parallel in mind, and tried
to avoid it. However, the two cases were different. In the Palestinian case, people fled
the West Bank in 1967 as a result of the "fear of physical harm and the psychological
pressure of dealing with the occupying army especially with regard to the honor of
women and the senior men" (Abdel Shakur, Mehanna, and Hopkins 2005:23). In
Egypt, people fled the Canal cities out fear of physical harm, yet they were not under
direct occupation of the Israeli army, such that they needed to be concerned with the
honor of women (Abdel Shakur, Mehanna, and Hopkins 2005:23). The similarity
can be seen in the fact that the Palestinians, in 1948, did not flee directly to a final
destination. Rather, they moved several times, and they even tried to get back to their
villages whenever they found a way to do so (Abdel Shakur, Mehanna, and Hopkins
2005:23). The same pattern can be noticed among the Port Saidians and the Suez Canal
migrants in general. None of them knew what to expect, yet they were thinking that the
migration would last only for a few months.

'Abduh asked the local administration of the city to take action against *al-aghrab* who obtained social housing units, leaving the genuine Port Saidians to suffer from the housing crisis. The writer emphasized that there were more than 1,500 Port Saidian families unable to return to the city because of the lack of proper houses. Several years later, in the April 1989 issue, a news report stated that the police director had ordered the demolition of the shacks in the suburbs of Port Said that were inhabited by people who had no work documents or children registered in the city schools. The article also mentioned a plan to survey all of the shacks in the city, to find any families with "fake claims" to rehousing and exclude them from the social housing plans. The order offered a reward of ten EGP for anyone who would report a newly built shack.

This account highlights the housing crisis in Port Said during the years of reconstruction, even a decade after the return to the city. The housing crisis reinforced the production of the legal identity of the Port Saidians and the illegitimacy of *al-gharib* (singular of *al-aghrab*). Earlier accounts illustrate clearly the image of the destroyed city that needed a lot of effort to be inhabitable again. The records of the local council of Port Said make it obvious that the administration was in a rush to meet the needs of the returnees. For instance, on 12 December 1975, the local council urged the administration to finish the preparation of the temporary shelter in the "socialist youth institute" as soon as possible. The local council also permitted landlords to add more floors to their existing buildings in the reconstruction areas after consulting the municipalities. On 17 March 1976, the council assigned two pieces of land to two different housing cooperatives and approved a governmental loan to a third one to finance the construction costs. Further, the council asked the department of electricity and drinking water to inform the residents of the power and water cuts schedule until the "phenomenon" of frequent cuts came to an end—hopefully soon. In April of that year, the council asked the members of the People's Assembly from Port Said to raise the issue of the repeated power cuts in the Assembly. In the same meeting, the council urged the administration to ask the Ministry of Housing to support the housing budget of Port Said with an additional one million EGP to meet the city's needs.

Together these fragments express the pressure of the returnees who did not wait for the reconstruction of the city. The desire to return to the home city after the tough years of *al-tahgir* pushed *al-muhaggarin* not to wait; the transitional period of *al-tahgir* had to come to an end. The conditions in the city made the Port Saidians more aware of *al-aghrab*, who were rendered mostly as opportunity seekers, according to the Port Saidians' accounts. This sensitivity intensified as the city's recovery time was prolonged. The housing crisis took a long time to be solved. The different accounts of various interlocutors made it clear that the al-Manakh neighborhood was full of shacks of *al-muhaggarin* who lost their houses.

Various factors contributed to this extension of the recovery time. In addition to the overall recession of the Egyptian economy starting from the 1970s, Port Said witnessed a permanent crisis in land management. The city is a semi-island, surrounded by water on three sides: the Mediterranean on the north, the Suez Canal on the east, and Lake al-Manzala on the west. These geographical barriers made it difficult to expand the area of the city, leading to a continuous increase in the prices of land and real estate. As Hajj Awad stated, "The land is so precious in Port Said." According to the Indicator of Deprivation in the Built Environment, an economic indicator launched in 2016 by a group of urbanists, Port Said has the least affordable houses in Egypt in relation to the average income of its residents. Furthermore, with the declaration of the Free Trade Zone in Port Said, more "strangers" arrived, more houses needed to be built, and more infrastructure needed to be expanded.

These factors could explain why the migration documents still play a role in identifying who is Port Saidian and who is not, even decades after *al-tahgir*. The employees in the social solidarity office made a point of complaining about the amount of work they had had to do during the last months, issuing certificates for all of the young men and women who wanted to apply for the new social housing apartments. It is still astonishing how the migration documents shifted from being related to a specific time to gain a sense of permanency, as if the migration had never ended. *Al-tahgir* here represents how the eventful could descend into the ordinary, the everyday, and how the effect of this critical event could last and haunt the present. Each time the social solidarity employee grasps one of these cards, the event of *al-tahgir* resurfaces. With the new use of these cards, the subjectivity of *al-muhaggar* is reproduced in the contemporary, fusing the migration and the post-return phases together, weaving the subjectivity of *al-muhaggar* with that of the "real Port Saidian."

It is true that the housing crisis after the return magnified the sensitivity toward *al-aghrab*, giving more weight to the claims of authenticity. However, the notion itself has roots in the prewar period. For instance, Radwan acknowledged that "the 'chauvinist pride' of the Port Saidian identity existed before *al-tahgir*, and not just after it, as most of the people think." He noticed this pride in various situations when he was young. "Families preferred a groom from a Port Saidian family over a stranger who just spent a few years in the city, although we are all strangers here," he explained. A groom from an established Port Saidian family was more trusted for marriage.

Also, in all elections, "there was a priority for the candidate who had extended roots in the city over the one who was a fresh newcomer," Radwan explained. He laughed while remembering the internal elections to choose the head of a community association of the immigrants from one of the Upper Egyptian villages: "They preferred a candidate who had spent more years in Port Said to another one who was a newcomer or had just spent fewer years in the city, although the newcomer had fresh connections to their roots in Upper Egypt." He explained that more years in Port Said means more relations with different circles, and a better ability to facilitate services. Radwan added another layer to the meaning of being a stranger (*gharib*) by saying, "If someone wanted to insult someone else, he said, 'You are a peasant.' Then the other one had to respond by saying, 'I am more Port Saidian than you.'" Being a peasant or *gharib* suggests a sort of cultural and social inferiority. Using the Latourian framework, *al-gharib* has to be created to facilitate the formation of the Port Saidians as a group, drawing a new borderline to define the self, acting upon the other (*al-aghrab*).

This is why it is not usual to describe the foreigners—that is, the non-Egyptians—in the city as *aghrab*. I never heard any of my interlocutors describing the foreigners who lived in Port Said until the 1950s as *aghrab*. They occupied a different and superior position in the city, or as it was stated by Eid, "The Frenchman walked as if there were a feather on his nose." The foreigners did not occupy the same position as *al-aghrab*. Although there were ambivalent feelings toward them, they did not seem like strangers to the city as the *al-aghrab* did. They could be hated or beloved, they even could be described as colonizers, but they were not *aghrab*. As several of my interlocutors mentioned, a lot of what constituted the distinctiveness of Port Said and its people was ascribed to the foreigners in the city—the Western clothing, the skillfulness of the workers, the openness to the world, and so on. Contrasting with *al-aghrab*, the foreigners were always rendered as part of what constituted Port Said, as my interviews showed. It is a selective, yet unintentional, process.

Several of my accounts attributed to *al-aghrab* a lot of "misbehaviors" after the return to the city, especially after the declaration of the Free Trade Zone. For instance, in the April 1983 issue of *The New Port Said*, an article talked about an anonymous businessman who kept breaking the law by bribing officials to facilitate his illegal work, especially smuggling. The magazine made a point of mentioning that the businessman was a stranger by adding, "Those strangers are responsible for the problems of the Free Trade Zone. There should be decisive actions to stop their continuous attempts to use bribes." As we will see in the next chapter, many of the undesirable aspects of the Free Trade Zone, such as smuggling, were attributed to *al-aghrab*. All of the city's changes were blamed on them, as stated by Eid:

> *Port Said in the old days was closed on its people. The houses were built with four floors, and that was enough. Now, the houses are 20 floors. Yet they are not enough for everyone [...] The Free Trade Zone brought three-quarters of the Egyptians to Port Said. The people did not find jobs in their cities, so they came here to work on anything. Now, Port Said is crowded with people who did not go through the wars we went through.*

The same act of othering can be found in the way the Nubian migrants encountered Upper Egyptians. As Mossallam (2012) states, there was a common saying among Nubians that reflected their feelings toward their new neighbors: *"Yakhudha temsah wala nigawizha fellah"* (She would sooner be taken by a crocodile than that we marry her to a fellah). Of course there are different contexts which shaped the relationships among Nubians, Upper Egyptians, and fellahin on one hand, and Port Saidians and *al-aghrab* on the other. However, in both cases the reasons are mostly related to cultural differences and economic unease.

During *al-tahgir*, the dream of the return to the city captured the imagination of the people. After the return, Port Said was not the same. After the declaration of the Free Trade Zone, Port Said "deviated" more and more from what it used to be. People who lived through *al-tahgir* were haunted more and more by the fantasy of "the return." It became an unfulfilled desire that takes different forms of expression, as discussed partly in this chapter and will be discussed more later. As previously mentioned, *al-tahgir* was more than an action of displacement or a temporary period of being distant from the hometown. Rather, it was a process of transforming the self, the other, the space, and the relations among all of them. It was a process that cannot be unpacked without weaving all of these fragments together: Hamza's visits to Port Said while it was under fire, Ghali's father's insistence on registering his newly born children as Port Saidians, the tendency of *al-muhaggarin* to stick together in clusters in the hosting cities, and the documentation process that produced the legality of the Port Saidians.

CHAPTER 3

Shifting Modalities: From Sea Trading to Land Trading

Port Said as a Place

One night, after finishing an interview in the al-Arab neighborhood, I walked along Saʻd Zaghlul Street, which cuts across two districts, al-Arab and al-Ifrang. It is one of the most commercial streets in Port Said, especially the part in al-Arab, which is full of clothing and home appliance stores. The weather was nice. Families were hanging out, looking in the shop windows. At the corner of one of the side streets, I found a small kiosk with a sign saying, "Mosques are the best places on earth, while markets are the most evil." The sign made me laugh loudly, especially because it was hung on a kiosk in the middle of the most commercial spot in Port Said. However, it resonated with what I heard repeatedly in various interviews, especially by those who are "anti-trading," or, more precisely, against the trading modality of the Free Trade Zone. People like Ghali, who is a *simsimiya* maker, and Eid, who is an artisan and a *simsimiya* poet, do not like the version of Port Said that emerged after the declaration of the FTZ. They think the dynamics that followed the declaration of the FTZ changed the city for the worse, made its people used to turning a quick profit, and altered the culture of the Port Saidians. There is always an ambivalent narrative toward the FTZ, even among people who work as tradesmen. It was common among my interlocutors to express contradictory positions toward the FTZ. "It helped the people to recover from the consequences of *al-tahgir*. However, it made the Port Saidians accustomed to quick profits. It was a gift from President Sadat to the people of Port Said, who suffered a lot. However, *al-aghrab* made profit out of it,

44

and not the locals." More contradictory statements about the FTZ were mentioned repeatedly in almost every interview that touched on the effect of the FTZ on the city and its people. The kiosk sign was no exception.

Port Said, as its name reveals, is a port city. It relies on activities related to the sea and to international marine traffic, among them trading. However, during my fieldwork, people were always pointing to the differences between the two modalities of trading, before and after the FTZ. The latter had a major transformative effect on the city and its people, although it started by a very simple act: the issuing of a presidential decree and the establishment of customs offices at the entrances of the city. This simple act triggered a complex chain of reactions that drastically changed Port Said. The shift from sea trading—*tigarat al-bahr*—to land trading— *tigarat al-bar*—can serve as an overarching label to describe these changes. Each modality of trading reproduced space and reassembled the social in a different manner, producing different subjects, documents, and systems of governance, adding more layers to a city that is always in the making. In this chapter, I follow the traces of these changes, unpacking their effects on the people of Port Said and the groups that were formed by the trading activities.

In this chapter, I rely on AbdouMaliq Simone's concept of people as infrastructure (2004), which was developed through his work on sub-Saharan African countries. He argues that people's activities in the city are part of the infrastructure that produces life. Through these activities, people are able to make cities functional, when otherwise they would be seen as "dysfunctional or incomplete." He argues that the people are able to engage complex combinations of objects, spaces, persons, and practices to reproduce life in the city. He gives as an example the transport depot of Abidjan, which is full of steerers, taxi drivers, baggage loaders, and the like. When a steerer approaches a passenger, he makes a quick assessment of his wealth, status, and needs. This helps the steerer to know where to take the passenger, who is the best baggage loader to load his baggage, and which taxi driver should take him. With no formal rules to guide them, all of these people in this heterogeneous network work together, relying on their knowledge of the space in which they interact. Simone elaborates that, through people's activities, specific spaces "are linked to specific identities, functions, lifestyles, and properties so that the spaces of the city become legible for specific people at given places and times" (Simone 2004:409). This collaboration and collectivity (and heterogeneity) open the possibility for the people to produce something in and with the city that is different from what is determined by the dominating powers, while still functioning within the same power domains.

Simone's argument can be linked to Michel de Certeau's explanation of space as a practiced place, differentiating between place as "the order in accord with which elements are distributed in relationships of coexistence" (1984:117) and space that is composed of the intersections of the movements of these elements, the relationships among them, the harmony and the contradictory nature of their movements. In that sense, "the street [as a place] geometrically defined by urban planning is transformed into a space by walkers" (de Certeau 1984:117). In general, de Certeau considered the everyday practices of the people within a certain space, the ways of operating, consuming, naming, using, and narrating these spaces, as ways not only to negotiate with the nets of sociopolitical discipline but to reproduce the spaces by consuming them. The practices that contribute to the reproduction of space are not merely the physical practices that interact with the physical space. They can also encompass practices like telling stories, naming places, and narrating the past, which even includes movements. While narrating the past, we move through time. When these stories about the past are told or recalled while wandering in the same locations where they took place, the movement becomes a movement through time and space. Stories about places and narratives about the past bridge various times and spaces, fusing them into new social and spatial realities.

Working in the Canal

"Like a boat in the water" is how the Captain described Port Said, emphasizing two facts: the city's attachment to the sea, and the geographical nature of Port Said as a semi-island. The first time I saw the Captain—or al-qubtan, as most people called him—was during one of the weekly nights of the al-Tanbura simsimiya band. When the band started to sing the al-bambutiya[1] song, he stood up and started to perform the folkloric

---

1 *Bambutiya* is the name of a specific group of tradesmen who use boats to reach ships in the harbor or while crossing the canal to get aboard and sell/exchange goods with the sailors and passengers.

dance of *al-simsimiya*, using his hands to imitate *al-bambutiya* moves, throwing an imaginary rope to an imaginary sailor on an imaginary ship. The rope was supposedly transferring a pack of something, such as a box of cigarettes, to the imaginary sailor. The latter took the box and tied money to the rope. *Al-qubtan* imitated the rope-pulling move to take the imaginary money. Later, he started another move, mimicking a boatman paddling with a small boat, while he moved his legs as if he were walking in the same place. Although he was 72 years old, he was dancing enthusiastically in his dark sunglasses and black navy cap. He was very famous to those who attended al-Tanbura concerts every Thursday night in the al-Nigmah casino in Port Fouad. The title *al-qubtan* referred to his job as a boatman in one of the companies of the Suez Canal Authority. His job was to go out to ships that had technical problems in the middle of the canal, allowing a team of technicians to help them. Secretly, he was also a *bambuti* (singular of *al-bambutiya*), which means he was selling commodities to sailors or exchanging goods with them on ships, while they were crossing the canal or docking at the harbor. Working as a *bambuti* was not illegal in itself; however, as an employee of the Suez Canal Authority he was not permitted to do it.

Al-bambutiya is one of the most traditional professions in the Suez Canal cities, and it is related to sea trading. In Port Said, it emerged during the early years of the city. The name is believed to be derived from the English word "boatman," as I was told by different interlocutors. It is used to describe sea traders who board ships while they are crossing the canal or docking in the port in order to sell goods to sailors, using small boats to reach the ships in the middle of the water, and rope ladders to climb aboard. The goods that were sold ranged from oriental gifts and souvenirs from the Khan al-Khalili in Cairo, clothes, wristwatches, and leather goods, to larger items such as home appliances, which needed bigger boats to be conveyed and a couple of men to help the *bambuti* to lift them. Working as a *bambuti* requires more skills than being an ordinary trader on land. It requires knowing other languages to communicate with sailors from everywhere on earth, good bargaining skills, a sharp mind to know what kind of goods suit which ship, and good connections with the port officers and the Suez Canal employees in order to know the marine traffic schedule. From the maritime traffic office, *al-bambuti* can learn how many ships will arrive on a certain day and at what time. Then, from the shipping agency office, he can find out how many crew members will be on each ship, their nationalities, their destinations, and how long they have been at sea. Based on this information, he can estimate the type and quantity of merchandise he can offer to these ships, and the number of assistants he needs. This network of relationships is part of the human infrastructure through which the city operates, as laid out by Simone (2004). Through these networks, massive amounts of information are exchanged and circulated every day. Based on this information, quick assessments and decisions are made by *al-bambuti*, who then engages other networks of assistants, suppliers, and boat owners (from whom *al-bambutiya* rent the boats they need to convey their merchandise). These networks and ways of operation have been developed over decades of practicing this profession, becoming more complicated with time and resulting in the formation of *al-bambutiya* as a group in the city.

Working as a *bambuti* was a source not only of money, but of connections with people, as I was told by my interlocutor Azzam, who practiced the profession for decades. *Al-qubtan* recounted, "During my childhood, when I found chicken leftovers before one of the houses, I assumed that there was a *bambuti* inhabiting this house," referring to the fact that only *al-bambuti* could afford a chicken meal. Yet money was not the only source of value in this job; relations with foreigners was another reason that people admired it. While I was sitting with *al-qubtan*, he pointed to his navy cap and told me that he received it as a gift from an American navy sailor while his frigate was crossing the canal. He also took from his pocket a red napkin with the words "Made in the USA" on it despite the fact that it was actually made in China, telling me that he bought it from an American sailor. For *al-qubtan*, these tiny belongings kept him connected to an imagined adventurous world, to a worldwide brotherhood of sailors who at some point crossed the canal. He continued to speak proudly about different gifts and goods he managed to get from sailors, such as Swiss knives, jackets, suits, and watches. He sold some of these things, and kept others for himself as evidence to be shown to someone like me, as a proof of being connected to this world.

Azzam, who is 59 years old, also told me about his father, who spoke English, Dutch, and Greek, which increased his ability as a *bambuti* to communicate with sailors of different nationalities. He did not learn these languages in school; he acquired them in the course of practicing his job, as most of *al-bambutiya* did. During my interviews, Azzam and *al-qubtan* kept using scattered English words in the middle of their sentences, to assert their knowledge of foreign languages. The social capital of *al-bambutiya* was premised on their relationships with the port officers, the Suez Canal employees, and the foreign sailors and captains they knew. They could not practice their job without the various relationships that facilitated their work. The gifts they received from the foreign sailors were a reward that added to the value of this social capital.

Azzam inherited his job as a *bambuti* from his father, who likewise inherited it from his father. *Al-qubtan* also inherited his relation to the sea business from his family. His father owned a small boat, which he leased to *al-bambutiya* or shipping agencies. The rest of his family members were working in the harbor. "All of my family members were working in the sea. What could I have been expected to do on land?" he wondered. Although *al-qubtan* perceived himself as an heir to his family's work, Azzam was literally a legal heir to his father's *bambuti* license, which carried the number 334. Each *bambuti* has to have a license to practice his work and a permit to have access to the port and the ships. Azzam showed me his license, which was issued by the Ministry of Transportation, and two permits: one to access the port and the other to get aboard the ships. It is written on the license that it is valid only for three years, after which it has to be renewed. The other two permits have to be renewed every year, according to Azzam. This technique allows the state to control who is allowed to enter the harbor, through periodic reviews of the criminal records of each *bambuti*. The boatman may lose his license if he is convicted of a crime, or misbehaves on one of the ships. The licenses can be inherited by *al-bambuti* family members. So Azzam inherited his father's license, one of his brothers inherited the grandfather's license, the second brother inherited the grandfather's brother's license, and the third obtained a new license as a recognition of his courage in the 1973 war.

Starting from the mid 1970s, the state ceased issuing new licenses, which resulted in a decline of the number of *al-bambutiya* from 600 to 396, according to Azzam, who was also the head of the Sea Traders Association until 2012. The association was established in the mid 1950s "to organize the work, and to maintain the custom of their profession," as Azzam explained. There are also other associations for *al-bambutiya*, such as the Trade Union for Sea Traders and the Sea Trading Association. "One of the rules is to ensure that, when a *bambuti* gets aboard a ship, he knows the language of its sailors. This is why I work on Russian ships, while my father worked on Dutch ships," he explained. This rule is imposed not only to ensure efficiency but also to avoid conflicts among *al-bambutiya*.

Figure 6: A picture of a *bambuti* license that was issued in 1957.

Besides *al-bambutiya*, there were other groups (*tawa'if*) that worked in ship services, such as the ship waste group that bought scrap from ships and sold them to scrap merchants. There was the artisans group, which includes hairdressers, ironers, smiths, and carpenters, who boarded ships to provide these services. All of these individuals needed licenses to practice their jobs and permits to enter the harbor and board ships. They had their own organizations, similar to the Sea Traders Association, to represent and organize them. There were other extinct groups, such as coal heavers, that disappeared as shipping technology developed.

The daily lives of these *tawa'if* were connected to the marine traffic, but they were not alone in this. "The whole city was ready for foreign visitors," as Hajj Awad described Port Said in the past, adding, "The city relied on tourism and trading activities related to the canal." The golden decades of sea trading in Port Said lasted until the 1960s. During this time, the city was full of souvenir shops, restaurants, casinos, bars, and hotels to serve foreign sailors and tourists who were crossing the canal, as well as foreign residents in the city. Hajj Awad's family was part of this life. They owned several shops in Port Said, where he started to work when he was young. He was born in 1950, and started to work while he was in primary school. He did not continue his education after middle school, preferring to work with his family. For Hajj Awad, trading was more attractive than being hired by the government or even working for the Suez Canal Authority. "What I was earning from trading in a month was double the salary of an employee in the Canal Authority," Hajj Awad explained. At that time, ships were required to wait in Port Said's harbor until they received permission to traverse the canal in a convoy. "The ships would line up, starting from the statue of Ferdinand de Lesseps [at the beginning of the wharf] and extending to the Customs Department gate," Hajj Awad recalled. During the waiting time, sailors and tourists were permitted to enter the city, companies supplied ships with their needs, and *al-bambutiya* provided their commodities. Before the eventual spread of phone lines in Port Said, one person's job was to wake up people who worked in ship services, notifying them that a ship had arrived and telling them in which part of the harbor it was docked. His job title was *al-mosahati* (the man who wakes people up). He traveled by bicycle, with a list of names and addresses of people he needed to wake up for work. The city sprang to life whenever ships arrived, as Eid described: "When we had ships in the port, the al-Ifrang neighborhood would stay lit up until the morning."

The accounts of these men describe a life that was centered on the sea. And by "the sea," or *al-malih* (the salty) as the Port Saidians describe it, I mean both the Mediterranean and the canal, as most of my interlocutors merged them into one entity. *Al-malih* was the source of wealth and the base of the existence of Port Said's people. The city was purpose-built as a port, located in this spot to be the terminal of the canal. In that sense, the canal was more than an object; it was an agent that contributed to the assembling of the social and the production of the space of the city. All of the *tawa'if* were social groups that formed around the canal and its activities. The rhythm of the traffic in the canal controlled the rhythm of life in Port Said, as if the canal were a maestro conducting its orchestra. Before going to Port Said, I had thought of the city as a space with two major poles of activities: the Free Trade Zone and the Suez Canal Authority, but I was wrong about the Canal Authority. The canal is bigger than the institution. The various modalities of lives connected to the canal are more complex and too broad to be confined within the boundaries of the Canal Authority. The canal was perceived as something that belongs to the people of the city and not to the authority that runs it. The canal defined the existence of the people who were related to it. There were many more people who were related to the canal than just the ones who worked for the Authority.

Before the nationalization of the Suez Canal in 1956, the possibilities for Egyptians to obtain jobs in the Suez Canal Company were limited. Those who succeeded were less privileged than their foreign colleagues. Even so, people were admired for the fact that they worked for the company. It was a source of social prestige, a stable salary, and a sustainable job, especially for those who were not from merchant families. "When we saw someone riding a bicycle, we knew that he was an employee of the company," Eid explained, talking about residents of the al-Arab neighborhood. At that time, few people owned private cars or bicycles. The majority walked or took cabriolets (horse-drawn carriages). The sole public bus line moved along Kisra Street in the al-Arab neighborhood, as Eid explained, emphasizing the smallness of the city, on one hand, and the dichotomy between the residents of al-Ifrang and al-Arab, on the other. Generally, the number of employees in the Suez Canal Company was very small in proportion to the city's population. Eid remembered applying for a job at the company in 1955, and although he passed the work tests, he was not hired because he was Egyptian. The rule was to wait until another Egyptian employee died or retired and then to hire another as a replacement. In July 1956, 1,028 employees and pilots were working in the company, 453 Egyptians and 557 foreigners, according to the Suez Canal Annual Report of 1958 (Suez Canal Authority 1958:28). Eight years later, the number had jumped to 10,174 employees (9,776 of them Egyptians), with the establishment of new factories and companies related to marine services, as mentioned in the Suez Canal Annual Report of 1964 (Suez Canal Authority 1964:116). Eid was among those who were hired by the Canal Authority after nationalization. *Al-qubtan* was working for one of the private companies that provided services for ships while crossing the canal. In the 1960s, his company was nationalized, among other private companies, and merged with the Canal Authority. All of these actions increased the significance of the Canal Authority in the economic lives of the people of Port Said. Yet the activities related to the canal were more numerous and diverse than the Canal Company or Authority. The canal's activities always affected more people than just the ones who actually worked in its official institutions.

Drawing on Latour (2005), we can here follow different actors who produced the port as a juncture between the outside world and Port Said, such as *al-bambutiya*, who moved continuously between the port and the city, with the canal as a passageway linking different parts in the world. These ceaseless movements transformed the port (the place) to a juncture, a space of intersection among the local, the national, and the global, where people who were related to sea trading developed their identity and sense of belonging to the world. The space is produced through these movements and everyday operations, as was explained by Lefebvre (1991) and de Certeau (1984).

My interlocutors define themselves through work, lifestyle, clothing, and small belongings like *al-qubtan*'s possessions. All of them related in one way or another to the sea. Even the self-perception of the Port Saidians was linked to the sea—both the Mediterranean and the canal, both of which are mediators to connect Port Said with the world. Ghali, the *simsimiya* maker, emphasizes the effect of the sea clearly by identifying the sea as the source of a set of characteristics that distinguish the Port Saidians from *al-aghrab*, such as desiring liberty, refusing discipline, and hating restrictions. For instance, it was common among the Port Saidians to see themselves as not fitting in jobs that require discipline. Ghali was working in the prison of Port Said as a supervisor of the woodcrafts workshop, but he resigned because he could not tolerate its restrictive rules. He preferred to devote his time to his carpentry workshop and *al-simsimiya*. Ibrahim, the son of Hajj Awad, never liked his job in the petrochemical factory. He disliked the strict routine of factory life, especially since he had previously worked in trading since he was young, but he shifted to an industrial job as a result of the recession in Port Said after the 2011 revolution.

For people like Azzam and *al-qubtan*, the sea enabled them to inter-weave their lives with people from other places in the world, increasing their social capital. Azzam was proud to tell me about captains he knew from Russia. "*Al-bambutiya* is a worldwide profession. I saw *al-bam-butiya* in all of the port cities I visited, in Turkey, Greece, and Russia. I would sit for hours, watching them while they were working," Azzam gladly explained. The same pride and joyfulness could be seen in *al-qubtan* when he spoke about the souvenirs he got from foreign sailors. For both Azzam and *al-qubtan*, working in sea trading gave them a life that had a new face every day, which is not the case in the repetitive daily routine of working at a factory like Ibrahim.

The Free Trade Zone

Al-tahgir was a moment of rupture with the sea trading modality. The forced migration laid the groundwork for land trading, which evolved with the declaration of the FTZ. During the *tahgir* years, people were not able to practice their work. They were away from the space that allowed the sea trading modality and shaped their lives in the way they knew. Although this was also the case in Suez and Ismailiya, the long-term effects of *al-tahgir* and the declaration of the FTZ transformed the city and reproduced it in quite a different way from what it was before, as will be explained in this chapter. In March 1976, President Sadat issued Decree no. 24/1976 to declare Port Said a free trade zone. The decree was constituted of two articles. The first one declared the whole city to be a free trade zone, starting from January 1976, and authorized the president to issue subsequent decrees to regulate it. The second article was an order to publish this decree in the Official Gazette (*al-Garida al-rasmiya*), putting it into effect from the day after its publication.

This was not the first time that establishing a free trade zone in Port Said had been contemplated. In 1964, the minister of finance issued Decree no. 117/1964 to authorize the governor of Port Said to declare free trade zones in specific places in Port Said, allowing imported goods to be traded in these zones without adding customs fees. How-ever, only foreign visitors were allowed to buy the commodities in these zones. Between 1965 and 1967, several decrees were issued to allow diplomats, Egyptian citizens who lived abroad, and employees of inter-national organizations to buy commodities from these zones. In 1966,

Legislation no. 51/1966 was issued to establish a free trade zone in Port Fouad, with the intention of gradually expanding it to the whole city. However, with the outbreak of the 1967 war, the project was halted. Nor was Port Said the first city in Egypt to have a free trade zone. In 1956, the economy and finance minister issued Decree no. 2 establishing the first free trade zone in Egypt within the port of Alexandria. Other decrees were issued in the same year to establish free trade zones in the transport depot of Alexandria and in the Cairo Airport's terminals.[2] However, all of these cases were limited in their capacity to transform the spaces they were located in. They aimed mainly to attract more foreign currency to the local market.

Drawing on Harvey (1989), the declaration of the FTZ can be explained as part of the shift from managerialism to entrepreneurialism, which emerged as a recurrent theme in the advanced capitalist world beginning in the 1970s. Harvey explains this shift as a general consensus that "positive benefits are to be had by cities taking an entrepreneurial stance to economic development" (1989:4). He identifies three features of this shift, developed from his work on Baltimore but applicable generally to other cities as well. First, entrepreneurialism has the notion of "public–private" partnership, "in which a traditional local boosterism is integrated with the use of the local government powers to try and attract external sources of funding new direct investments, or new employment sources." Secondly, this public–private partnership is entrepreneurial because it is speculative rather than being rationally planned and coordinated. Thirdly, the entrepreneurialism focuses on the political economy of a specific place rather than a whole territory (Harvey 1989:7).

Traces of the same shift can be found in the case of Port Said. The idea of the FTZ in Port Said was to attract private investments to the city, hoping that they would help to reduce unemployment, generate money in the market, and generally help to deal with the recession of the 1970s. The declaration of the FTZ was speculative to the extent that the decree that founded it consisted of only two articles, as was previously mentioned, and the governing rules of the FTZ were not declared for another 22 months, with Law no. 12/1977 (Mohamed

---

2   For more information about the Free Trade Zone in Port Said and other cities in Egypt, see Mohamed Abbas 2001.

Abbas 2001:262). Finally, the declaration of the FTZ addressed the political and economic issues of a specific city, and not as part of a national plan.

The declaration of the FTZ allowed the import and sale of duty-free goods within the borders of the zone. Port Said was franchised to import duty-free goods with a specific quota, to avoid a negative impact on the national economy. Two main customs offices were established at the southern entrance of Port Said, al-Raswa, and the northwestern entrance, al-Gamil, where people's belongings were inspected by police to estimate the required customs duty for the imported goods they had bought. A new extended network of relations was interwoven as a result of the FTZ. Most of the Port Saidian tradesmen who had become impoverished during *al-tahgir* were not able to start their businesses directly. However, some of them managed to do so. "Some people borrowed money from banks to import goods, while others borrowed money from family members or people they knew," Hajj Awad explains. At that time, Port Said attracted businessmen from outside the city, Egyptians and even Syrians and Lebanese, who started partnerships with Port Saidians. Gradually, changes were triggered by the money that was injected into the market. Wholesalers started to buy commodities from importers, and retailers started to buy from wholesalers, selling goods to small stores and street vendors. Consumers from everywhere in Egypt flooded the streets of Port Said to buy foreign commodities, which were seen for the first time after almost two decades of Arab Socialist policies. Hamza, who was mentioned in the previous chapter as the owner of a fish restaurant, said that buses from all over Egypt would stop close to the train station. The area around the train station was full of visitors and street vendors. He opened a small fish restaurant there. The whole city, especially the al-Arab neighborhood, turned into a market, where anyone could start a business selling perfumes, clothes, fruits, chocolates, home appliances, even cars.

A person did not need either a large amount of capital or a formal place of business to start trading in Port Said. Ibrahim, the son of Hajj Awad, preferred to be independent of his family. He decided to sell clothes on the beach to summer visitors. However, his father asked him to do anything else but this work, saying, "It is the work of *al-aghrab.*" So Ibrahim started to work as an independent vendor. He neither owned his goods nor worked for a specific person. Instead, he was like a middleman, attracting the client from the street to a store and selling him goods after adding his profit to the price. Then he paid back the original price of the commodity to the owner of the store, keeping his profit. The amount of money he earned depended on his bargaining skills. He was working for himself, enjoying the ability to establish his terms of collaboration from one shop owner to another. His capital was the ability to convince the client to come and see the goods in this store or that, reaching a good deal with him. To do this, he had to make a rapid assessment of each client to estimate what he or she needed and how much money the client could pay. This is how people work as infrastructure, through these connections between middlemen and shop owners, adjusting their offers to the clients according to quick assessments that have no written guidelines (Simone 2004).

Although I did not visit Port Said during these golden years of the FTZ, it is easy to imagine the city based on a popular movie that was filmed there in 1981. The name of the movie is *al-Mashbouh* (The Suspect). It is about a thief who decides to give up thieving after coming too close to being arrested by a police officer. He gets married and decides to move to Port Said to work in trading there. He obtains a small amount of capital to start working as a street vendor. In one of the scenes, he stands in one of the streets of the al-Arab neighborhood behind a table full of clothes. Everyone in the market is shouting to attract clients to the merchandise. Although the movie did not focus primarily on Port Said and the FTZ, it emphasized the fact that if someone wanted to start a business somewhere with a minimum of capital, Port Said could be just the place to do so.

Beside the commodities market, there was another market for import permits, or *bitaqat istiradiya*, the state documents that franchise specific persons to import goods worth a specific amount of money. These are import permits, specifying the value of the goods that can be imported every year. The limits range from US $2,400 to 66,000. Since Port Said as a whole had been assigned a specific quota for imports, the number of permits was limited. It increased from time to time whenever the import quota for Port Said increased, which has always been a matter of contestation between Port Saidians on one side, and other non–Port Saidian businessmen on the other. Starting in 2002, Port Said's import quota was decreased several times by the government, ushering in an epoch of recession in the city that has continued until now (Saleh 2012).

Not every permit holder chose to take advantage of his permit himself. Instead, some of them passed their permits to other people, who used them to import goods under the name of the original owner. In other words, the import permit became a commodity in itself. The exchange value of the permit was determined by various factors, such as its original value and the economic conditions of the market in Port Said. A permit with high value could provide its owner a fortune every year that enabled him to stop working. Over time, brokers started to appear to facilitate deals between permit holders and buyers, as did all the middlemen who appeared in each process related to trading in Port Said. There was a story that was repeated each time I interviewed anyone about the FTZ, about a belly dancer from Cairo who owned an import permit worth one million EGP without being either Port Saidian or a trader. Regardless of the truth of the story, it was told to indicate to what extent the permit market grew even beyond the borders of Port Said.

Smuggling was another facet of the FTZ. Imported commodities were not allowed to leave the FTZ without paying the required customs duties. However, controlling the borders of the whole city was almost impossible. "Smuggling started with the beginning of the FTZ. Having customs offices means having smuggling activities. It is the rule, not only here but everywhere," Hajj Awad explained. The government authorities attempted to stop smuggling by building a wall by the shore of Lake al-Manzala. However, it was difficult to keep the lake under surveillance 24 hours a day, seven days a week, especially since the lake was used for fishing and fishing boats were used for smuggling. In the opinion of my interlocutors, smuggling sabotaged the FTZ. It deprived Port Said of its advantage of being the source of foreign commodities, allowing them to leak out. They blamed it on *al-aghrab*, "who did not care about the city." For my interlocutors, smuggling was of no use to the Port Saidian merchants, who already benefited from the FTZ and had no interest in sabotaging it. On the contrary, *al-aghrab* might not have a "place" in the city, so they did not mind participating in smuggling, regardless of its destructive effect on Port Said.

When one of my interlocutors mentioned that *al-gharib* (the stranger) might not have a place in the city, he did not explain exactly what he meant. However, the vagueness of the word "place" disclosed the meaning more than any other word. "The place" here is anything that could be a source of ownership of, and belonging to, the city, a place with which to identify. *Al-gharib* was presented as someone who does not belong because he has nothing to identify with in Port Said; he is seen as rootless. Customs officers, who were accused by my interlocutors of being involved in smuggling activities, were also described as *aghrab*, who sought to be relocated from other cities to Port Said so they could make money from smuggling. "For them, Port Said was like the Gulf countries," one of my interlocutors emphasized in a sarcastic tone, referring to the migration waves of Egyptian workers and middle-class professionals to oil-rich Gulf countries during the economic depression in the 1970s and 1980s.

Ahl al-qimmah (People on the Top) is another movie produced in 1981. Ali Badrakhan, the film's director, was known for his critical views toward the *infitah* (open-door economic policies). The movie was based on a novel by the Nobel Prize winner Naguib Mahfouz. It was, again, about a thief, one who was working for a businessman from Cairo. The thief, named Za'tar, traveled to Port Said to facilitate smuggling on behalf of the businessman, who was using his import company as a cover for his illegal activities. Za'tar was doing most of the risky work, such as bribing customs officers and removing valuable smuggled merchandise from Port Said in a truck. Eventually, he accumulated enough wealth to start his own business. He established an import company, recruited other thieves from his past life, and continued in the smuggling business. In one of the scenes of the movie, Za'tar tries to justify his actions to his fiancée: "I turned poor thieves into rich people; this can happen only through a revolution. But I did it in my own way."

The stories in these two films resonate with the stories of the belly dancer, the smugglers, the consumerist spirit that reigned in Port Said, and the changes in the Port Saidians' culture as it was described by my interlocutors. Together, they constitute a narrative about the "dirty money" that dishonored the land trading modality. Behind the moral judgment on land trading's morality, this narrative reflected an unease toward the FTZ and its effects on the city, although a large number of people made a profit out of it. I believe that this unease evolved after the destruction of the FTZ, which led to a catastrophic situation in Port Said, as will be explained in the next section of this chapter.

The FTZ triggered massive social mobilization in the city, allowing people from the most deprived classes to become wealthier. As Hamza described it, "Those who succeeded in accumulating money were almost barefoot at the beginning." The transformative capacity of the FTZ was empowering on the one hand, and destructive on the other. Most of my interlocutors held that the FTZ made people used to quick profits, spreading consumerism among Port Saidians. "People were making money from the FTZ to spend on Cairo nightlife. During the weekends, you could see the lineup of the Port Saidian cars in al-Haram Street in Cairo in front of the nightclubs," one interlocutor said in a resentful tone. Furthermore, people abandoned their crafts to work in trading. "Now, we recruit craftsmen from other cities. The FTZ vanished but people forgot everything about other crafts except trading and smuggling," Eid said sorrowfully. This was why he did not like the FTZ and its effects on Port Said and its people. Ghali, too, refused to work in trading. He admitted that he wanted to try working as a tradesman during the FTZ period, but decided to stick to his carpentry craft. For him, it was safer and more honorable. People would never stop needing a carpenter, whatever happened.

Sea Trading in the FTZ

The declaration of the FTZ was just one of the factors that negatively affected the sea trading modality. At the beginning, the FTZ afforded *al-bambutiya* more commodities that could be sold on ships. However, with time, fewer people became interested in the *bambutiya* profession; land trading became more profitable. Another factor affecting the *bambutiya* profession was the halt in issuing new licences, which led to a decrease in the number of *al-bambutiya*, starting in the 1970s. More was said on this subject in *The New Port Said* magazine. In the April 1983 issue, an article by a Port Saidian parliamentarian discussed the negative effect of the construction of a new bypass to the east of Port Said that allowed more ships to enter the canal without stopping in Port Said's harbor, shortening the waiting time for these ships but negatively affecting the sea trading activities. Further, after the 2011 revolution, most of the ships ceased to stop at Port Said's harbor. Instead, they preferred to dock in the Mediterranean while they waited for permission to transit the canal. Companies were afraid of letting their ships wait in the harbor due to the lack of security in Egypt during that time. This resulted in reducing the number of ships that *al-bambutiya* could board each day. Even when ships did dock in the harbor, an increasing number of captains refused to let *al-bambutiya* on their ships, to avoid conflict between them and the sailors. Azzam said that the "outsiders" who invaded the *bambutiya* profession in the last years were the reason for the increasing troubles on ships. He implied that the police officers favored these outsiders, and let them work in the harbor without the *bambuti* licenses, because of the "services" they had provided for the police in previous times or because of their relations with the police officers in general. Azzam believes that most of the people who now work as *bambutiya* see it merely as a source of money. "No one cares any more about relationships as we did in the past," he explained.

Tourism has also been affected in recent years. Starting in the 1970s, tourism agencies altered the business by organizing pre-scheduled programs for foreign passengers to visit tourist places outside Port Said, instead of letting them wander the city freely. Since that time, the city has ceased to attract foreign tourists. Azzam remembered sadly how, in October 2016, a huge cruise ship with thousands of passengers and crew members docked in the harbor, raising hopes that Port Said would see a return of the old days. An employee from the tourism agency decisively refused to let the passengers and the crew members step outside the harbor, insisting on taking them directly, in company buses, to catch up with their tour schedule, although officials from the harbor and the police headquarters tried to convince him to let the tourists visit the city.

The new modality of trading reassembled the social in a different manner. Land trading was not arranged through family ties as had been the case in the sea trading modality. For instance, while most of *al-bambutiya* inherited their licenses from older family members, land trading was more open to anyone, even non–Port Saidians who moved to the city specifically for this reason. Starting in the 1970s, the target audience of trading shifted from foreign visitors to Egyptians from other cities, who went to Port Said to buy imported commodities. Land tradesmen (street vendors, middlemen such as Ibrahim, importers, newcomers to Port Said) and local visitors to Port Said were new actors who reassembled the social in a different way, reproducing the city as a space that is not associated with the sea as it was in the past. Port Said is still a port city. But the meaning of the port altered from being the junction between the city and the world to a mere gateway for imported commodities, which ceased to have the same value as the gifts and goods that were given to and exchanged with *al-bambutiya* during their work on ships. The imported commodities became detached from the social relations that produced them as fetishized commodities, while the gift gains its value from these relations. The red napkin of *al-qubtan* is valuable not because of its exchange value, but because it is evidence of this relationship between *al-qubtan* and the foreign sailor, the city and the sea, the local and the global.

Space also was reproduced in a different way, with new spatial practices and movements. Over time, gift shops, casinos, bars, and hotels started to disappear, especially with the emigration of foreigners from Port Said, which started in the 1950s. The trading hub moved from the harbor and the al-Ifrang district to the al-Arab neighborhood, ushering in a spatial transformation of the city. Al-Ifrang lost its centrality in favor of the al-Arab neighborhood, which became the center of the city. With the decay of sea trading and the rise of land trading, trade shifted from being a way to communicate with the world to being an affair confined to the local. For sea trading, mobility was part of the modality, while in land trading, confining mobility was the core of the modality. Sea trading depended on the mobility of ships in the Suez Canal and the wandering of foreign visitors in the city, while land trading depended on preventing imported commodities from exiting the FTZ, using walls and gates at the entrances of the city. The imported cars that carried licenses of the Free Trade Zone were not allowed to stay outside Port Said for more than 90 days each year. They were valuable duty-free commodities. They had to be confined within the city borders. Each time a person took his car to get out of the city, the police officer at the gate recorded the exit date in a small record, which was to be kept with the driver. Later, the officer would record the entry date, ensuring that the total time the car spent outside Port Said did not exceed 90 days. To expand the time that the car was allowed to be outside the city, its owner could buy a new record after finishing the first one. It was an irony that being a "free city," as part of the *infitah* policy, meant more control and confinement.

With the shift from one trading paradigm to another, a sense of disorientation haunted those who were attached to the decaying sea trading modality. For them, the city had become unrecognizable. Azzam explicitly expressed this feeling of disorientation. "I was a *bambuti* for 26 years. And now I feel that my life has gone in vain." Azzam preferred now to stop working as a *bambuti*, leaving his position in the Sea Traders Association, and devoting his time to helping his son run his clothing shop. Azzam travels every month to Turkey, using his connections there to import clothes to his son's store. Although *al-bambutiya* did not disappear, the profession has become marginal in the current era. It lost its value as a way of connecting its people to the world through the sea. Now, *al-qubtan's* belongings are mere debris of the sea trading modality, which was swept away. When *al-qubtan* was performing the *bambutiya* dance, he himself became the ruins of the life of sea trading. The dance became the monument of sea trading. He and his dance were reduced to mere folklore that belongs to the territory of the past.

Land traders have also known their share of disorientation. Although I did not visit Port Said during the golden years of the FTZ, I can sense the vibrant life of the al-Arab neighborhood through my interlocutors' accounts about these years. I can see the streets full of visitors and vendors, and the queue of cars and buses at the gates of the city waiting for the customs officers to inspect them. I always heard these stories from my older relatives about their trips to Port Said, in the 1970s and 1980s, to buy foreign clothes and home appliances before marriage. Port Said was the destination for many middle-class families to buy the things they needed. The city now looks totally different. Trading is dead after years of recession and consecutive decisions to decrease the city's import quota. Port Said has lost its advantage as the source of imported commodities. Now one can buy whatever one wants in any location. The economic recession following the 2011 revolution added more wounds to the city. I walked through the al-Arab neighborhood, in the same streets that in the past were busy with selling and buying. Now the streets are devoid of visitors. I was walking alone in an open museum of mannequins located on the streets, outside the shops, displaying clothes that had no buyers. Even the traders showed no interest in attracting me to their merchandise. The grids of al-Arab looked like an open museum of a destroyed life that was transformed into rubble of the past, as explained by Gordillo

(2014).[3] I asked Ibrahim, who had to change careers to survive, "If the situation gets better, will you go back to trading?" He replied:

> *Nothing can make the situation better. The state can prolong the life of the FTZ, as it already does, by renewing its import quota. However, this will not make any difference. The increasing value of the US dollar will affect the prices of the imported commodities. The poverty of the majority of Egyptians will not allow them to buy anything with the current expensive prices. At the beginning, the FTZ was providing commodities that were not found anywhere else in Egypt. Now, you can find everything everywhere. Why would anybody come to Port Said?*

The death of land trading in Port Said is reflected in the reckless attitude of customs officers at the gates of the city. During my repeated visits to Port Said for five months, my bag was inspected just once, as if everyone agrees with Ibrahim: trading in Port Said is dead. Everything is mere rubble now, from the market and the gates to the land traders themselves.

---

3 For Gordillo, rubble is the debris of the past that disrupts the present time. It signifies a life that was swept away or destroyed. He distinguishes between rubble and ruin, as the latter is the fetishized past, the attempt to turn rubble into something that merely belongs to the past and has nothing to do with the present. This concept will be discussed further in chapter five.

CHAPTER 4

Al-Simsimiya Has a Story to Tell

We are al-bambutiya.
No one is like us.
We are the sea traders,
working in the canal.[1]

Al-Simsimiya Performances

In mid-November 2016, I wrote in my field notes that I was naive at the beginning to have neglected following *al-simsimiya* during my visits to Port Said. Initially, I had designed my field research to focus mainly on the modalities of trading, the different patterns of relationships with the state, group formation, and spatial transformations. However, with time, the field started to lead me through the loci of the remaking of Port Said. *Al-simsimiya* is one of these loci. I wrote in my field notes:

> It is not accidental that Ghali, who wanted to identify himself with a specific narrative about Port Said, decided to tie himself to the making of simsimiya. He always describes the real Port Saidian as honest, life-loving, and liberty-seeking, instead of an opportunist who seeks quick profit. He associated the latter with the Free Trade Zone and its effects on the city. Also, Ghali attributes what he perceives as the real Port Saidian to the sea. Simsimiya maintains the same narrative about Port Saidians. I could not find a song about the Free Trade Zone, although there are songs about bambutiya, fishermen, al-tahgir, the resistance during the 1956 war, love, and life. This silence says something.

I wrote these lines admitting my naiveté the day after a *simsimiya* night with the al-Tanbura band, the biggest *simsimiya* band now in Port Said, in al-Nigmah casino. It was my first time to attend one of these

---

1 From the song "Ehna al-bambutiya" (We are *al-bambutiya*).

Wednesday-night performances. The band was founded in 1988 by *al-Rayis* Zakariya (Chief Zakariya). The idea was to revive the art of *simsimiya*, after about a decade of decay. In the past 30 years, al-Tanbura has succeeded in bringing back old *simsimiya* players and singers and introducing new ones. After the 2011 revolution, new bands were established in Port Said, reviving the golden years of *simsimiya*.

When I told the taxi driver to take me to al-Nigmah casino, he smiled and asked me, "Are you going to attend the *simsimiya* concert?" I said "yes" with a smile too. I did not know the time of the concert, so I arrived an hour and a half early, to find the casino empty. For years, al-Tanbura used to organize these Wednesday nights on the shore of the Mediterranean in Port Fouad. There were no tickets or reservations. The audience just paid for their drinks. The band did not make any money out of these regular concerts. It was just a matter of keeping the rapport with the audience. Besides these nights, al-Tanbura participated as the main *simsimiya* band in the celebrations of 23 December[2] and Spring Festival[3] in Port Said.

---

2 Victory Day, on 23 December, is the anniversary of the retreat of the last soldier of the French and British armies from Port Said in 1956, after the Tripartite Aggression against Egypt that followed the nationalization of the Suez Canal by the Egyptian state. The day was chosen to be the national day of Port Said. Every year, popular celebrations take place in the streets of Port Said, where *simsimiya* instrumentalists and singers perform songs related to the civilian resistance during the 1956 war. Usually, other bands from Suez and Ismailiya also participate in the celebration.

3 Spring Festival, or Sham al-Nissim, is believed to be the oldest festival in Egypt. It is celebrated on the day after Coptic Easter. In Port Said, an observance called the Allenby ritual takes place on this day. Every Easter, dummies of different figures are made and burned in bonfires. The tradition is believed to date back to the 1920s, when people started to burn dummies of Lord Allenby. However, every year local artists choose different political figures to be burned in the festival. According to Alia Mossallam, the targeting of Lord Allenby may be linked to his role in containing and suppressing the 1919 revolution while he was the High Commissioner of Egypt between 1919 and 1925. Mossallam adds, "With time, his story seems to have lost significance, as people have come to refer to life-size dummies as 'Allenbies,' not always knowing who Allenby was." At Easter 1957, British generals of the 1956 war were the new Allenbies. Mossallam also mentions that she was told by some respondents that some of President Sadat's ministers were made as Allenbies after the enforcement of the open door economic policy. It is difficult to list the figures that were chosen to be the Allenby from the 1920s until now. However, most of the people I talked to remembered that Israeli leaders such as Moshe Dayan and Ariel Sharon had been selected at various times. I remember in 2003, with the American invasion of Iraq, George W. Bush was an Allenby. The Egyptian government has tried to stop the ritual of burning Allenby, claiming that it is a threat to public safety.

The chairs of the audience were lined up in rows to face the stage where the band would sit. The band was present in its full capacity this evening. Almost twenty members were sitting in a U-shape: two *simsimiya* musicians, four drummers, 11 singers, and *al-Rayis* Zakariya in the middle. The casino was full of people from different generations and classes, with a majority of men but also families that included women and children. As the performance proceeded, the audience started to interact with the musicians. On the right side of the casino, there was a group of old men; a friend told me that "they are loyal fans who always occupy this spot on Wednesday nights." One of them was clapping his thick palms enthusiastically and seriously in a constant rhythm without missing a beat. When the band started to sing the "We are *al-bambutiya*" song, another man from the same group stood up and entered the band's area to dance, despite his age and his huge belly. People often entered the band circle to participate in an enthusiastic dance, blurring the borderline between the musicians and the audience, while other people simply greeted some of the band members and sat beside them. Several times, the singers themselves stood up and started a spontaneous dance without any sort of organized steps. The act of blurring the borderline between the realms of the musicians and the audience eventually made it difficult to differentiate between the two groups of people.

The voices of the audience were rough, unlike the normal singing voice, while the voice of *al-simsimiya* was sharp, and the rhythm of its music was fast, leading to an adrenaline rush, pushing everyone to clap their hands excitedly with the rhythm. The dancers mimicked the moves of the *bambutiya* and the fishermen with their hands, while moving their legs quickly. For most of the evening, *al-Rayis* Zakariya sat in the middle of the band, with his charismatic facial expression, bushy mustache, and bald head. After each song, the singer would hand him the microphone. He would choose the next singer and hand him the microphone. The rhythm of the performance accelerated until the moment when Zakariya took the microphone to sing the last song. When he stood up, it was a sign that the night had come to its end. The audience praised him passionately, then listened to him sing the last song of the night.

After the 2011 revolution, former president Mubarak, Zakariya 'Azmi (former chief of presidential staff), Fathi Surur (former speaker of parliament), and Habib al-'Adli (former interior minister) were chosen to be the Allenbies (Mossallam 2012:126).

In this chapter, the focus will be on understanding how *simsimiya*, as a genre of music that requires a high level of sociability, contributed to the making of the social in Port Said. We will also examine the kinds of narratives about the city that *simsimiya* sustained—not only as a musical style but as an actor in the Latourian sense. In that sense, *simsimiya* could be seen as a storyteller that tells the history of the city, although not in the form of information as in a historian's work or a journalist's daily reports. Rather, it is in the form of a story, an experience that is full of affects. As Walter Benjamin explains (1969b), in this context it is experience that the storytellers draw on, not information.

For Benjamin, history is not the homogenous and empty time that historicism assumes. On the contrary, it is the rupture that can disrupt the now-time, opening the possibility for redemption. Historicism constructs history as a thread of moments that always move in a progression and are moved by it. For historicism, the past is a bygone moment that can be studied simply in its position in the thread of time. It belongs to another territory that has nothing to do with the now-time. Benjamin argues against this perception of history. He sees the possibility of seizing the past "only as an image which flashes up at the instant when it can be recognized and is never seen again" (Benjamin 1969a:255). For him, the past can exist in the present, in the current instant. He says, "To articulate the past historically does not mean to recognize it the way it was. It means to seize hold of a memory as it flashes up at a moment of danger" (Benjamin 1969a:255). Benjamin was trying to emancipate history from the concept of progression, perceiving the notion of progress as part of the claiming of history by the victorious. He calls instead for another history: historical materialism, a concept forged by Marx focusing mainly on the voices of the oppressed in history, making it vivid and alive in the present. In this way, the past can be emancipatory as long as it disrupts the present, and can open up to new possibilities.

A Brief History of *al-Simsimiya*

Al-simsimiya is a popular local collective singing genre in the canal area. It started in Port Said in the 1930s, according to Eid and *al-Rayis* Zakariya. It was preceded by another genre, *damma*, which means "the gathering" in Arabic. *Damma* was another kind of collective singing, influenced by Sufi music. *Damma* songs varied from Sufi to platonic love songs. It gained its name from the act of gathering, when working men gathered at the end of the workday in the house of one of them and sang *damma* songs in a slow rhythm, accompanied with tambour and sometimes a triangle. Over time, some of the singers gained a reputation as *damma* shaykhs, and became popular in the city. They were asked by families to sing on special occasions, such as marriages and pilgrimages. These men were not professional singers, earning their living from *damma*. Rather, they were workers and artisans who practiced *damma* out of love for this genre and its social rituals.

Despite the antagonism between *damma* and *al-simsimiya* in the beginning, the latter inherited many of the *damma* specificities. In order to understand the differences and similarities between them, I visited *al-Rayis* Zakariya in al-Mastaba cultural center for folkloric arts in Cairo, which he founded. *Al-Rayis* Zakariya is a Port Saidian artist with a leftist intellectual background. The cultural center has a small sound recording studio and a library of audio recordings of *damma* and *simsimiya* songs. He devoted years of his life to collecting and recording the songs and the music of *damma* and *simsimiya* from the shaykhs in the Canal city.

According to the oral narratives that *al-Rayis* Zakariya collected, Port Said was introduced to *simsimiya* when the Nubian musician Abdullah Kabarbar arrived in the city in the 1930s, carrying his *simsimiya* instrument. It is believed that he emigrated from Upper Egypt as part of the migration waves that followed the heightening of the Aswan Dam, leading to the flooding of some of the Nubian villages in the south of Egypt. He moved among the Canal cities, teaching people how to use *al-simsimiya*.

In Port Said, Kabarbar found his first followers among musicians who were practicing *zar*, which is a sort of healing music that invokes the supernatural powers that are believed to have control over human bodies. At that time, Sudanese and Nubians were famous for being able to help others find peace with these supernatural powers, healing souls and bodies through their ritualistic music. *Zar* people used the *tanbura*, an instrument quite similar to the *simsimiya* but larger, with a deeper sound.

Kabarbar found his first followers among *tanbura* musicians. They became known as *sanagiq*[4] (plural of *sunguq*). He started to teach those

---

4 *Sanagiq* are the people who play the *tanbura* during *zar*. I was not able to find the origin of the word.

who were interested in learning *simsimiya* techniques. However, Kabarbar and his followers were not able to reach an audience. *Damma* was dominant at that time, preventing anything new from taking root. Hence, Kabarbar started from a peripheral space, al-Makhanah, the Port Saidian hashish café. For *damma* people, *simsimiya* was inappropriate, associated with hashish and disreputable people, opposite to the spirituality of *damma*. They refused to include *al-simsimiya* and its people in their gatherings, protecting their domination of the sphere. But with the Tripartite Aggression against Egypt during the Suez crisis in 1956, *simsimiya* gained enormous momentum. *Damma*, with its slow rhythms and heritage songs, was not able to keep up with the events, while *simsimiya* was faster, and untrammeled by heritage. New *simsimiya* songs were able to reflect the intensity of the moment, playing the dual roles of boosting morale and documenting the history of the battle for Port Said, as in the song by Mohamed Abu Yusif, "Ya Port Said ya shabab wa rigal" (Oh, Port Said of Youth and Men).

> *It was a British conspiracy, planned with French deliberation,*
> *With the Jews they were a gang conspiring*
> *For seven nights and a morning.*
> *With planes and tanks they charged; their failed attacks fell hard,*
> *And we with our guns defended,*
> *For seven nights and a morning.*
> *They blocked the canal and nothing passes through.*
> *They cut off water, the light too.*
> *Life's become difficult and weary,*
> *These seven nights and a day.*[5]

That was the moment when *simsimiya* had enough power to replace *damma* and inherit its position.

During the 1956 war, singing *simsimiya* songs was compared to the writing of history, as described by Mossallam (2012). Mossallam relied on songs and oral history interviews to reassemble the narratives of this moment in Port Said. She writes, "[The singing of songs] is something

---

5 "Seven nights and a morning" was the duration of the bombing of Port Said between the night of 31 October and the morning of 7 November, during the Tripartite Aggression. The lyrics of the song were translated by Mossallam (2012:93).

[the singers] do collectively to bring different aspects of events together. Respondents also compared it to 'the making of history' as they attempt to assert and create political stances through their singing" (Mossallam 2012:91). Some songs documented specific events during the war, as in Eid's song about the soldier Sa'id Hamada, who was the security guard of the Italian consulate. When the British raids on Port Said intensified on 5 and 6 November 1956, the Italian consul asked Hamada to come inside the consulate building to protect himself. However, Hamada refused to leave his position, and died as a result. Eid, who started to write songs and poems in 1956, wrote this song to commemorate Hamada's courage:

> *Listen to this story of a soldier of freedom,*
> *Son of our country, the martyr, Sa'id.*
> *He stands with his arms firm to his sides,*
> *Protecting the foreigners in his country . . .*
> *The Italian consul in all his humanity*
> *Called to Sa'id, "Come in for safety!*
> *Save yourself from the carnage,*
> *And to your courage we will always be indebted."*
>
> (Mossallam 2012:114)

Drawing on Khalili's (2007) work on mnemonic narratives, which was also mentioned in chapter two, it can be argued that the heroic identity of the Port Saidians was forged through *simsimiya* songs. On 23 December of every year, the al-Tanbura band organizes a street performance in the al-Arab neighborhood to celebrate Victory Day, recalling these moments through songs about the people's struggle and fight for their city and families. The annual rituals of remembering this moment of victory have been repeated over the last 30 years to maintain the heroic identity of the Port Saidians.

What helped to sustain this identity was the fact that the battle of Port Said was integrated in the official narrative of the state. The heroic narrative about the Port Saidians helped to avoid questioning the military failure to protect the city from invasion (Mossallam 2012:89). On the other hand, the Port Saidians "relate their battle to the greater battle [against imperialism], and their community to Nasser's greater framed imagined community. Not, however, without emphasizing their own politics which drove and continues to drive their political activism" (Mossallam 2012:89). The struggle of the Port Saidians during the Tripartite Aggression, and the songs that represented these struggles, produced Port Said as an icon of resistance in the national imagination. Besides the popular celebration, there is also an official one. I was told by different interlocutors that Nasser and Sadat attended ceremonies in Port Said every year on 23 December, opening new projects in the city. There is also the Military Museum in Port Said that commemorates the popular resistance in 1956, yet without forgetting to underline the "state leadership" of this resistance.

On the other hand, the popular resistance in Suez against the Israeli occupation of Sinai between 1967 and 1973 did not occupy the same position in the national imagination. As Mossallam states:

> *There are, however, no monuments, statues, or museums in Suez and little documentation marking the popular struggle that began in 1967 and lasted until 1974. There is no commemoration of the defeat in 1967 and those who died fighting under poor leadership, nor of the 101 days of popular resistance that followed the October 6 "victory."*[6] *It is as if the state has made no attempt to impose a fragile narrative of its defeats and victories lest it risk the possibility of having to recognise or accommodate the narratives of the people of Suez.* (Mossallam 2012:207)

In the narrative about the popular resistance in Suez, *simsimiya* songs, which were produced by the *simsimiya* singers and musicians in Suez, represent an alternative narrative to the hegemonic one, produced by the state, which focuses merely on the "military victory" in the 1973 war. In both cities, *simsimiya* plays the role of the storyteller who tells the story of the city and its people.

During the 1950s and 1960s, *simsimiya* became the mainstream music in Port Said, inheriting the collective nature of *damma*. It even adapted some of the *damma* songs and readjusted its melody to *simsimiya's* fast rhythm. Gradually, *simsimiya* singers and musicians started to be asked to join family occasions, such as marriages and pilgrimages.

---

6 For more information about the popular resistance during the 1973 war, see Mossallam 2012:chapter 6.

Among the Port Saidians, certain families built a reputation as *simsimiya* families, such as al-Basous, Gamal ʿAdmah, Abu al-Morsi, al-Rayis al-Dash, and al-ʿAshri. Members of these families took part in *simsimiya* nights, which used to be known as *dammit al-simsimiya* (the *simsimiya* gathering) or *sohbit al-simsimiya* (*simsimiya* companionship). Abu Islam, a contemporary *simsimiya* musician and singer, told me that *al-mosahati*[7] used to go around on his bicycle, inviting the *simsimiya* people to join the *simsimiya* gatherings. Until that moment, *simsimiya* was not a profession. The players were workers, artisans, truck drivers, *bambutiya*, and the like. It was part of the social life of the Port Saidians. Singing took place in cafés, family occasions, and street performances. *Simsimiya* families played the major role in developing the form by providing it with poets, instrumentalists, and singers. Although playing *simsimiya* required talent, most of its performers were illiterate (Mossallam 2012). Songs were transmitted by memory.

Within the specific forms of sociality that were created around *simsimiya*, such as *dammit al-simsimiya* and *sohbit al-simsimiya*, people formulated different relations with themselves and with each other. Outside these gatherings, they were ordinary people working in different fields, and might not have any direct relation to each other. Within the *simsimiya* gatherings, their personalities gained an additional layer: the layer of the singers. With *simsimiya* songs, they could be heard and noticed. What connected them to these gatherings was the ability of *simsimiya* to transform them into someone else. There is a common word to describe the act of participation in these gatherings, *nistihaz*, which literally means "to gain luck." It is related to another common expression, *saʿit haz* (an hour of luck). Hence, the time they spend in the *simsimiya* gatherings is *saʿit haz* (an hour of luck) and what they do there is to gain luck. Both expressions describe the gathering as an exceptional time, different from their ordinary lives as workers, artisans, and truck drivers. This is the reason why most of the *simsimiya* gatherings are organized at night, after the working day.

One of the *simsimiya* gatherings that I attended was in al-Makhanah. Ghali accompanied me to the place, saying that he thought it would be more useful for me to meet the *simsimiya* people in their

---

7 *Al-mosahati*, mentioned in chapter three, had previously gone around on a bicycle to inform the people that there was a ship docked in the harbor.

natural place rather than setting up a meeting somewhere else. Al-Makhanah was just like other cafés, a small place with a limited number of wooden tables and chairs. It was still early, and the place was almost empty, but after an hour, customers started to occupy the empty chairs. Ghali took me to a specific table on the left side of the café, where a group of five men were sitting. These were the members of the Sawt al-Karawan *simsimiya* band. The band was established in the late 2000s by Abu Islam, who was born and raised in a family of musicians. Three of his uncles were *simsimiya* musicians. During the 1970s and 1980s, he was trained by the *simsimiya* shaykhs. Like all of the members of the band, Abu Islam was not a professional singer; he did not make his living from singing. He had been a worker at one of the companies of the Suez Canal Authority since the 1980s. After the long working day, the members of the band gathered in this café to entertain themselves. "Here, we sing for ourselves. The best singing we do is in gatherings like this," Abu Islam said. The band also organized public concerts in Port Said, but the times closest to their hearts were when they sang for themselves.

The waiter was moving between the tables with *shisha* loaded with hashish. Each person at the table took several puffs before handing the *shisha* to the next person. After several rounds, the singers and players were ready to begin. Abu Islam started to sing and play on his *simsimiya*. People in the café joined in by clapping their hands. In each song, there was a main singer and the rest of the band repeated the lyrics after him. In the next song, another member would be the main singer, the others would be the choir, and so on. Everyone had his chance to play the leading role for a couple of minutes. For each singer, this was the moment to remember, the moment that goes beyond the ordinary. Following the Latourian framework, *simsimiya* in that sense is an actor. On one hand, it contributes to the making of the social through allowing forms of sociality, and on the other, it contributes to the production of the subjectivities of the musicians.

Al-tahgir affected *simsimiya* deeply by spreading it among the Port Saidians. In every place to which the Port Saidians emigrated, a *simsimiya* band was established. The immigrant bands, as they were named at that time, were singing mainly for the rubble of the city, clinging to the hope of returning to Port Said one day, as in this song by Eid.

Oh, the city of the lighthouse and the canal!
Oh, the city of the strength and the struggle!
Oh, Port Said, my home!
Oh, Port Said, my home!
I stand here protecting my canal,
I stand here protecting my sand.
I pass by the doors,
waiting for the return of my neighbors.
Oh, Port Said, my home!
Oh, Port Said, my home!

As mentioned in chapter three, Eid was one of *al-mustabqayin*, who remained in Port Said to run the necessary services for the army. In this song, he was singing for *al-mustabqayin* who stayed to protect the city, waiting for their neighbors to return. Another song by Eid paints a picture of the abandoned city before *al-tahgir*, remembering how it was before the war.

My heart livens up
when it sees a building
beside another building.
It cheers up
when it sees a garden
watered by a man's hand.
I like to see ships,
while they are
loading and unloading.
I adore the sound of the sea,
its breath and sand,
while sitting in sunshade,
watching a kid
collecting seashells. . . .

I grieve for
the abandoned factories,
the dark houses,
people without smiles,

without souls,
waiting for the hand
that will revive their lives,
knocking on their doors. . . .

Be strong, my country,
in tough years;
the hope persists.

"*Simsimiya* was the friend who consoled us in our tribulation," *al-Rayis* Zakariya said, describing *simsimiya* as an actor or an agent that stood beside them in the tough years. During *al-tahgir*, more people started to join *simsimiya* bands, while new generations of poets were born. Even among *al-mustabqayin*, new bands were established. Eid formed his *simsimiya* band, Shabab al-Nasr (the youth of victory), from those who stayed in Port Said. He wrote lyrics and composed music. The members of the band had never performed *simsimiya* before; they were members of the National Guard and the civil resistance.[8] The main musician of Shabab al-Nasr was Abdallah al-Amerikani, who worked for the military hospital in Port Said. "We were singing for the soldiers and *al-mustabqayin* in the summer theater on the shore of the sea, in the state cultural palace of the city, in the workers' club, and in the military camp," Eid remembered.

Later, the band started to travel through the cities of the Nile Delta, singing for *al-muhaggarin*. "We visited al-Mansura, Tanta, Damietta, al-Mahalla, and al-Matariya, singing for our people, consoling them and raising hope that we would return to our city one day," Eid said. During *al-tahgir*, *simsimiya* became the connection with the distant city, and a reminder of the life that had been left behind. That life was not wiped away, but was waiting for the people to re-inhabit it. For *simsimiya* people, their city and their life existed as long as the people remembered it through their songs.

Analyzing this using Benjamin's work (1969b) on the storyteller, we can say that *simsimiya* was a storyteller who told *al-muhaggarin* the news of their city and of *al-mustabqayin*, reminding them of their lives before

---

8 Paramilitary troops that were organized by the state during the time of the 1956 and the 1967–1973 wars to protect the city.

al-tahgir. Drawing on Latour (2005), *simsimiya* can also be viewed as an actor who is not only telling stories and transmitting experiences, but also contributing to the production of *al-muhaggarin* as Port Saidians, through their involvement in singing from time to time. *Simsimiya* was the thing that reconnected *al-muhaggarin* to the city they were far away from. The metaphors in the songs worked as vehicles, bridging spaces that separated the Port Saidians from their city. In de Certeau's terms (1984), singing was a spatial practice that took place every day, affording *al-muhaggarin* short visits to Port Said, reproducing the latter as home. The absence of the city was converted to presence through *simsimiya* songs.

The popularity of *simsimiya* among Port Saidians during *al-tahgir* laid the groundwork for establishing professional bands after their return to the city in the 1970s. For Abu Islam, "the leap of *simsimiya* started with the declaration of the FTZ. People started to be richer. More wedding ceremonies were arranged in the streets of the city, which resulted in increasing the demand for *simsimiya* from people who were able to pay." In his view, this helped *simsimiya* bands to develop. Each band started to have its own poet and composer who produced new songs, enriching the heritage of *simsimiya*. Some of these bands, such as Hassan al-'Ashri's, gained wide popularity among the Canal cities. He even produced cassettes, and some of his songs were broadcast on the radio. Abu Islam kept moving among these bands, attempting to learn from each one of them.

However, this success did not last for long. Zakariya said it lasted merely for a few years after the return. Starting from the late 1970s, the famous *simsimiya* figures retired one by one, and no new songs were produced. When I asked Abu Islam about the reason for this retreat, he was not able to give an explanation, but *al-Rayis* Zakariya suggested that it was the result of the commercialization of *simsimiya*. In his opinion, the bands started to focus more on earning money from wealthy people than on producing art. Ghali thought it was a shift in audience taste that led to abandoning *simsimiya*; people like Hassan al-'Ashri and other *simsimiya* figures stopped working when they sensed the wind of change. What remained in the market was the "commercial *simsimiya*," which focused mainly on earning money from singing for wedding parties, and the state-sponsored band that performed in the cultural palace of Port Said, mainly on official occasions such as Victory Day on 23 December. It turned *simsimiya* into mere folklore, detached from the social life of the people of Port Said as it was in the 1950s and 1960s.

In 1988, al-Tanbura started its long process of reviving *simsimiya*, forging a different path. *Al-Rayis* Zakariya attempted to maintain a sort of independence for his band by avoiding being commercial. In the first years, he managed to finance his band from his own money and savings, depending on the revenue from a workshop he had owned. He did not want to charge money for their performances, so as to avoid being affected by market forces and the desires of the people who owned the money, as he put it. He succeeded in convincing some of the retired musicians to join al-Tanbura, and paid them a monthly salary. The old musicians started to teach new volunteers, transmitting knowledge to them. People started to learn about the band by attending its weekly rehearsals, which turned into weekly concerts, such as the one I attended in al-Nigmah casino. Over time, al-Tanbura built its audience in Port Said. Then it started to perform in other cities and villages in Egypt.

Over the years, cultural hubs and centers noticed al-Tanbura and invited them to play in Cairo. Zakariya managed to obtain grants from foreign cultural institutions, which helped the band to sustain its work. They began to be well known even abroad. They were invited to festivals in Paris, London, Berlin, and other cities around the world. Locally, Zakariya refused requests to play at family occasions, although he continued to perform in al-Nigmah casino and in the street performances for Victory Day and the Spring Festival.[9] This approach was meant to be seen as a rupture with the commercialization approach in the 1970s, which was blamed for the decay of *simsimiya*. Other new bands took the non-commercial approach to a different level. Ghali and Abu Islam spent years in al-Tanbura before leaving it during the 2000s and forming the new band Sawt al-Karawan. In their conversations with me, they justified this split by saying that they became uncomfortable with the grant money, believing that money changed the dynamics among

---

9 During the 2011 revolution, al-Tanbura organized five *simsimiya* nights in Tahrir Square among the protesters. In the months that followed the revolution, the band participated in various concerts and activities in several governorates including Cairo, Alexandria, and Tanta. It called itself the "Lowest Council of Culture," mocking the state's Supreme Council of Culture (Kalfat 2013).

the band members. They were seeking ultimate dedication to *simsimiya*, and pure loyalty to the art, without any material benefits.

Al-Tanbura's non-commercial approach created a problematic situation. It was intended to protect the band from being a "wedding ceremony band" like the commercial *simsimiya* bands in the late 1970s—a term coined by Zakariya during our conversation. By commercial *simsimiya* bands, he meant the bands that played at wedding parties to encourage the wedding guests to give money to the married couple, by calling the guests' names, greeting them, and asking them to "salute" the married couple by giving them money, known as *noqtah*. The bands then received part of the *noqtah*, and that was their source of income. Zakariya thought this was a humiliating way to perform *simsimiya*, because "these bands, after a while, ceased to sing; they were just focusing on the process of collecting *noqtah*." This was why he refused to let al-Tanbura perform at family occasions. However, this decision prevented the band from being part of the social life of the Port Saidians, as *simsimiya* had been in its early years. Further, the involvement of al-Tanbura in the "culture industry" by performing in festivals and cultural hubs in Cairo made it similar to other bands, risking its spontaneity and sociality. Yet in the band's public and street performances, there are still traces of this sociality and spontaneity. In general, Zakariya attempted to sustain a critical position between two worlds: the world of professional bands who perform onstage and according to a prepared program, and the world of spontaneity, collectivity, and sociality of *simsimiya* that I saw in al-Nigmah café and the street performances.

After the 2011 revolution, more bands were established, following the same non-commercial approach. Besides al-Tanbura on Wednesday nights, there are other *simsimiya* nights in other places in Port Said. Suhba, which was founded in 2015 by a group of young *simsimiya* musicians, plays in one of the cafés on the Port Said seaside. Sawt al-Salam plays in the Sa'd Zaghlul public garden in al-Arab. Another band plays in the customs employees' club. On most of these nights, I found families attending the concerts. These bands do something more than provide entertainment. They open more spaces for the past and its narratives to be reproduced in the present, ignoring the period of the FTZ, despite the fact that the current non-commercial approach to producing and consuming *simsimiya* is indeed a reaction against what happened during the FTZ epoch.

This long story of *simsimiya* tells a lot about the city and the different ways in which it was produced. It could be said that *simsimiya* maintained a certain narrative about the city as the daughter of the sea and the canal, documenting the critical events in the life of the city such as the wars of 1956 (*al-ʻudwan al thulathi*) and 1967–1973, and playing a major role during *al-tahgir* as the locus of the reproduction of the city and its people. For people such as Ghali and Zakariya, who did not favor the FTZ, *simsimiya* was a point of departure to remake the city in their own way, linking it to the pre-FTZ period. *Simsimiya* had this ability to recall certain fragments of the history of Port Said, a past that was related to the resistance during the 1956 war, and the relations among the city, the sea, and the canal, skipping over the period of the FTZ with all of its complexities that were discussed in the previous chapter.

Ghali mentioned once that he was happy because more young men were now starting to value participating in activities such as *simsimiya* bands, which made him feel as if Port Said were reviving again. He even turned part of his carpentry workshop into a museum of *simsimiya*, naming it "al-Turathiya" ("heritage"). He collected old *simsimiya* instruments and hung them on the wall with information cards stating the year of manufacture of each one. Almost every time I visited Ghali I found a group of young *simsimiya* musicians and singers there, playing for themselves. This simple group action reinforces the existence of *simsimiya* in Port Said, along with all the narratives about the city and its people, reproducing these narratives materially by gaining more believers. Ghali eventually enlarged the museum by expanding a few meters into the street. He also organized an annual *simsimiya* gallery on a specific street corner in al-Arab during the Spring Festival. In this gallery he displayed old *simsimiya* instruments and sold new ones for beginners. He even manufactured small ones for children, hoping to encourage more people to learn how to play, and revive what he believes is the "real face of Port Said": the sea, the canal, and the resistance.

CHAPTER 5

Remaking the City after the Port Said Stadium Massacre

The Massacre and Its Immediate Effects

"February 1st, 2012 is a significant date in my life. Suddenly, being a Port Saidian became an insult, where before it was my source of pride." This is how Misho remembered the Port Said Stadium Massacre. The massacre was the most catastrophic event in Egyptian sports history. Clashes between fans of the al-Masry (the Port Saidian sports club) and al-Ahly football teams broke out in Port Said Stadium after one of the Egyptian League matches. Seventy-two people were killed and hundreds were injured, all of them members of Ultras Ahlawi, the biggest fan group of the al-Ahly team. The fights were preceded by several skirmishes between the two fan groups, as part of the rivalry between the football teams.

The incident was unprecedented not only in the number of victims, but also in its consequences. Al-Ahly fans accused both the security forces and the Green Eagles, one of the fan groups of al-Masry, of organizing and conducting this massacre against Ultras Ahlawi members, as a result of the latter's participation in the events of the 2011 revolution. Other political revolutionary groups shared the al-Ahly point of view, accusing the Supreme Council of the Armed Forces (SCAF), the ruler of the country during the post-revolution period, of organizing the massacre. The event took place a year after the toppling of Mubarak's regime. During this year, the police and military repeatedly used deadly force to suppress massive demonstrations calling for change, leading to the death and injury of protesters, which made the accusations against

SCAF even more convincing—especially since members of the Ultras Ahlawi were always part of the groups protesting against police and military brutality. It was a moment of shock across the whole country. The police director of Port Said and the governor of the city resigned, the national football league was suspended, and clashes between al-Ahly fans and police troops lasted for almost a week on the premises of the Ministry of Interior in Cairo. The hardest part for the Port Saidians was the stigma that the event placed on them.

Misho, with whom I started this chapter, was studying architecture in Cairo. He is a basketball player, and a socially popular person. He was born and raised in Port Said. He had no difficulty finding a place for himself among his colleagues in the architecture school in Cairo. He was well liked until the massacre, when a radical change occurred in the way people dealt with him. He was blamed for the massacre, just because he was Port Saidian, as he told me. Some of his colleagues stopped talking to him. Others dealt with him brusquely. "I did not understand this attitude from people who knew me!" Misho remembered. He was surprised by the tendency to accuse every Port Saidian of being responsible for the massacre. "Actually, there were a lot of Port Saidians who sympathized with the al-Ahly fans," Misho claimed. He found it painful to follow the media coverage, which was quite aggressive toward Port Said and Port Saidians, especially sports media. Misho remembered when "a player from the al-Ahly football team insulted all Port Saidians on his Facebook page by saying that they were cowards when they fled their city during the war." Misho was verbally harassed by one of the teaching assistants in the university, which resulted in an altercation between them in the classroom. For Misho, the issue was how to convince people that "Port Said is not merely the massacre." He did not find the answer at that time, yet he kept searching for something he could do.

I was told a similar story by Ahmed al-'Ashri, the founder of Suhba, one of the new *simsimiya* bands established in Port Said after the 2011 revolution. After the massacre in 2012, he was invited with al-Tanbura to participate in the al-Fan Maydan ("Art Is the Square") conventions, a monthly cultural event that started after the January 2011 uprising and continued until 2013. It was organized by several cultural groups and initiatives, with the main idea of organizing a musical event in one of the main squares of Cairo. Later, the event took place in different cities at the same time every month, until the security forces started to obstruct it after the fall of the Muslim Brotherhood regime in July 2013, an event that was followed by several acts to control the public sphere.

Al-'Ashri remembered the moment when al-Tanbura was introduced by the organizers of al-Fan Maydan. There was a storm of disapproval among the audience, which came mainly from the corner where a group of al-Ahly fans had gathered, as he remembered. They were shouting and asking the band to leave the stage. However, the band started to sing and their performance was outstanding. Al-'Ashri remembered that the audience praised them enthusiastically at the end of the concert, which convinced him that art can make a difference. It can convince people that "Port Said is not merely the massacre." The same phrase, although articulated differently, was used by both Misho and al-'Ashri.

The stadium massacre made most of the young people of Port Said feel attacked and stigmatized, called "thugs," "perpetrators," and "criminals." I was told by a Port Saidian friend that there was a rumor circulating in Port Said that people in Cairo would attack any Port Saidian car if they noticed its licence plate from the FTZ. Regardless of the truth of the rumor, it showed how deep the effect of the massacre was. The stigma was an act of othering the Port Saidians, and as a reaction, they started to "other" those who were othering them.

As a Cairene, I experienced this type of othering in February 2013 when I visited Port Said for the first time. As a journalist, I was covering the massive protests against the death penalties that were issued on 26 January 2013 against the Port Saidian defendants in the stadium massacre. Police troops opened fire on the families and supporters of the defendants, which led to another massacre among the protesters who had gathered in a spot close to Port Said prison. The defendants were perceived as innocents who were sacrificed to satisfy al-Ahly fans. During my visit, I met many angry people who described the trial as unjust. They thought that the government was trying to placate the al-Ahly fans because there were so many of them. During the year between the two massacres, the Ultras Ahlawi managed to organize huge protests in Cairo, where most of its members were. Indeed, the al-Ahly fan protests proved capable of paralyzing Cairo, worsening the situation for the Port

Saidians, who started to view the death penalties as a matter of compromise from the government, "which does not care about anything except the people of the center, Cairo," an opinion that was heard several times in Port Said.

During my visit to Port Said at that time, I was easily spotted because of my camera. I was repeatedly stopped by people in the streets and suspiciously asked about what I was doing there, and for which media outlet I was working. For example, one young protester accused me of defaming the protesters by portraying them as thugs and perpetrators. Several times, the protesters forced TV crews to leave the area because of their lack of trust in any media channels from Cairo. There was a public mood of suspicion and even incitement against everyone and everything that represented "the others" who were associated with the act of othering the Port Saidian people.

This chapter will focus on the reproduction of Port Said after the traumatic experience of both the stadium and the prison massacres, by following several actors, mainly Misho and al-'Ashri. Both of them began initiatives connected to the past of the city: one is related to the architectural heritage of Port Said, and the other is related to *simsimiya*. Both initiatives will be viewed through the lens of Walter Benjamin's theses on history (1969a) and Gaston Gordillo's work *Rubble: The Afterlife of Destruction* (2014). The latter argues that the elite of any society have a sort of sensitivity toward rubble that remains from the destruction of the "old world" by the forces of colonialism, modernism, capitalism, neoliberalism, and the like. Rubble is a sign of wiped-away worlds. It always signifies a destruction that happened and needs to be hidden. Hence, the elite begin to make efforts to turn rubble into ruins. By "ruins," Gordillo means "dead things from the dead past, whose value originates far in time" (Gordillo 2014:9). Ruins separate rubble from the present, deprive it of the afterlife of destruction, and turn it into a mere fetish, a heritage that needs to be preserved and reserved. In this chapter, I engage with this argument, situating *simsimiya* and the old buildings of Port Said within this debate about ruins and rubble.

A Response to Civil Unrest

For more than a month after the death penalties were handed down against the Port Saidian defendants in 2013, the city rose up against the authorities. Protesters flooded the streets of Port Said. On the day after the prison massacre, tens of thousands of citizens participated in the funeral of the victims. The police troops attacked the funeral, which enraged the Port Saidians. The clashes continued in the city for three days. The number of casualties among the protesters reached 46. Soon, Ismailiya and Suez joined in the protests. The Islamist president, Mohamed Morsi, declared a state of emergency and enforced a night-time curfew in the three Canal cities, threatening those who attempted to "spread chaos." However, the protesters in all three cities challenged the curfew and the state of emergency by organizing not only night protests in the early hours of the curfew but also football matches as a way of mocking the presidential decree. Further, the Port Saidian protesters started a sit-in in al-Shuhada' Square (Martyrs Square) in front of the governorate administration building and the police headquarters.

The city descended into a complete state of rebellion by calling for civil disobedience. For weeks, marches were organized every day, moving across the whole city. Every morning, the protesters gathered in front of the main gate of the industrial area, blocking the road to prevent the workers' buses from entering the factories. The marchers then began walking down Mohamed Ali Street to al-Shuhada' Square, pausing in front of each school and government institution, asking the people to join them, or at least to show solidarity with the strike. I remember that one day, when the march passed the headquarters of the electricity company, the employees went outside the building with a sign indicating that they supported the strike. It was the employees' way of apologizing to the protesters that they were not able to leave their offices at that time. The march did in fact include many signs that carried the names of institutions, companies, trade unions, and syndicates supporting the strike.

With the declaration of the state of emergency, the military was ordered to restore order in the three Canal cities. However, it became obvious that the military did not want to put itself out in front of the people. In making this decision, it was taking a step back from aligning itself with the Muslim Brotherhood regime. Meanwhile, the police disappeared from Port Said. They hid inside their headquarters while people were reappropriating the streets. Graffiti and photos of the faces of the prison massacre martyrs were everywhere in Port Said. During the sit-in, the protesters established the "people's police station," where people could symbolically file reports against the political regime figures. The station consisted of a marquee in Mohamed Ali street. At the entrance, the protesters hung a sign reading "The state of Port Said— the Police Station of Mohamed Ali Street—the people in service of the people," inverting the slogan of the Egyptian police, "The police in service of the people." Inside the symbolic police station, the protesters hung a list of the names of those wanted for justice, including President Mohamed Morsi and the Muslim Brotherhood leaders Khayrat al-Shater, Mohamed Badi', and Mohamed al-Biltagi.

During the strike, people recalled the resistance against the Tripartite Aggression in 1956. One sign in the sit-in emphasized this link: "Port Said fought the Tripartite Aggression, and it will fight the Muslim Brotherhood." *Simsimiya* bands, including al-Tanbura, produced new songs about the prison massacre and the resistance of the Port Saidian people, comparing it to what had happened in 1956. In Walter Benjamin's terms (1969a), the Port Saidians were recalling specific fragments of history to disrupt the present. By recalling the history of resistance during the Tripartite Aggression while protesting police brutality, the protesters were drawing a parallel between the two moments, fighting back against the stigma that had attached itself to them after the stadium massacre. The city was characterized again as a rebellious city, but this time against suppression and marginalization. During my conversations with people in the sit-in, there was a deep sense of being marginalized, attributed both to the economic recession after the reduction of the import quota in the FTZ, and to the stigma against Port Said and its people after the stadium massacre.

The attempt to convince people that "Port Said is not merely the massacre" posed the question of what Port Said actually was. For al-'Ashri, the answer was found in *simsimiya*. As he told me, he focused on studying *simsimiya*, improving his skills, and connecting more with other young *simsimiya* musicians and singers. Before that moment, he was playing *simsimiya* as a hobby. His main focus had been on his studies and his work as a medical lab technician in a private hospital. However, after the al-Fan Maydan incident, he started to regard *simsimiya* as something important for himself and the city, without knowing exactly what this thing could be, or at least without being able to articulate it during our conversation.

One day during the summer of 2015, one of al-'Ashri's friends was drafted into the army. Al-'Ashri and some of his other friends decided to organize a *simsimiya* farewell party for him in one of the cafés by the seashore. Although they were singing for their friend without a sound system or proper equipment, people in the café treated them as if they were a band. Some of the audience filmed videos and uploaded them online, describing them as a new *simsimiya* band. People accordingly started to regard them as a new band, although al-'Ashri and his friends had not intended this. After that incident, however, they began to consider singing for the public by organizing concerts in the same café, and the owner of the café welcomed them. They called themselves the Suhba (Friendship) band, a name capturing their very basic idea as just friends singing for themselves. The café shared the profits from the *simsimiya* nights with the band. They used this money to purchase more equipment and uniforms. They have maintained this non-commercial approach until now. They use the profits strictly to improve the music and the appearance of their band. The regularity of the concerts, every Friday in the Jasmine café, accelerated the band's popularity. I attended one of their nights in September 2016—the first anniversary of the band. I was surprised by the number of middle-class families who attended the event. People were praising them as the new generation of *simsimiya* musicians who would keep this part of the history of the city alive.

For Misho, answering the question of what is Port Said took a different path. As an architect, he was interested in the architectural heritage of the city. Between 2012 and 2014, he started to collect more information about the unknown buildings of Port Said, such as the "International Hotel," which was the first hotel in the city, the old lighthouse, Casa d'Italia (the House of Italy), the guest house of Empress Eugenie, and others. He gathered his friends from the Ramses Club on the basketball court, and started to ask them about these buildings to raise their curiosity. "I realized that half of the Port Saidians walk in the streets staring at their feet. They do not see the buildings in front of them," Misho explained. He succeeded in increasing his friends' curiosity about these buildings and their histories by organizing several walks to visit these buildings, sharing what he knew about them. After the walks, they created a Facebook group to discuss how to help other people see these buildings. "The dream that captured us was to reopen the old cinema houses, renovate Casa d'Italia, make the streets clean again, protect the buildings with unique architecture from being demolished, and in general to restore Port Said as it was," Misho stated. They named their group Port Sa'id 'ala Qadimo (Port Said as It Was).

When I asked Misho about the reason behind this interest in architectural heritage, he replied that Port Said has a distinctive architectural style, which could be attractive to visitors. "This uniqueness and distinctiveness of architecture can make the city functional again," Misho explained, referring to the economic recession affecting the city. He is trying to suggest an approach that makes the heritage buildings profitable by renovating and reusing old places. He hopes that this approach will reinstate tourism in Port Said. His group has a plan for renovating Casa d'Italia and turning it into a center for cultural events. He believes that visitors from nearby cities such as Ismailiya, Suez, and Damietta will be interested in attending events there. Furthermore, the restaurants, cafés, and hotels around the renovated places will also benefit from the presence of the visitors. In this way, he was trying to interweave the heritage work with the normal lives of the people of the city, linking abstract notions such as "heritage" and "culture" to people's everyday life.

He tested this approach by organizing a trip to Port Said for 80 students of his university colleagues from Cairo. He arranged a walk in the city, a *simsimiya* concert, a lunch in a famous fish restaurant, and a deal with some clothes stores to give the visitors discount vouchers to buy clothes from these stores. For him, the most successful part of this trip, two years after the stadium massacre, was the positive feedback from his colleagues about Port Said. "My main aim was to change the bad idea of my colleagues about Port Said, to convince them that it is more than just the massacre. And I succeeded in this," Misho explained.

The Port Sa'id 'ala Qadimo walks were repeated several times. Each one added more buildings, stops, and narratives, thus fusing time and space more intricately. A walk through the space became a walk through time, following the different historical phases of the making of the city. Over time, more people, mainly students, joined the group, which now has 150 members. During the Spring Festival, they organize a week of walks and an exhibition of old pictures of Port Said. The exhibition takes place in front of al-Wasifiya, one of the oldest schools in Port Said.

I attended the exhibition in 2017. I stayed for almost an hour, observing the interactions of dozens of people who visited the exhibition. I noticed that most of the younger people were asking questions about the histories of the places, what happened to them, and how they changed through time, while the older ones were sharing their memories and stories about the same places. I talked with a man in his eighties from a middle-class background. He spoke of how "clean, organized, and beautiful" the city used to be in the past. In general, he perceived the past of Port Said as more "cultured, cosmopolitan, and civilized," with a variety of cinemas, theaters, and communities, than it is in the present. This type of nostalgic rhetoric was common among the older people who visited the exhibition.

In 2016, the group struck a deal with the owner of the Rio cinema house on al-Gumhuriya Street in the heart of al-Ifrang to renovate the lounge of the cinema, abandoned for years, and use it for art events. Port Sa'id 'ala Qadimo financed the renovation costs, and they now use the cinema for film screenings and music concerts. Another of the group's projects is to renovate Casa d'Italia, which was built in the 1930s by the Italian fascist government of that time. The front of the building still carries one of Mussolini's quotes. It is believed that the building was established initially to be the residence of the future Italian ruler controlling North Africa. However, the building was closed after the Second World War until now, with the exception of a few years during the 1980s when it was turned into a theater and cinema for a short time before it was closed again. Port Sa'id 'ala Qadimo made a proposal to the Italian consulate to reopen the building and use it as a cultural center. However, the consulate refused, because they could not reopen the building with Mussolini's quote on its front. They also pointed out that the building is in disrepair and cannot be used. Later, the consulate offered the building for sale. Yet Port Sa'id 'ala Qadimo still talks about the building and their plans for it in every event they organize.

When I asked Mus'ad, one of the organizers of Port Sa'id 'ala Qadimo's events, why certain places, such as al-Arab, had been excluded from their walks, he seemed not to have considered the matter before. However, he finally replied that most of the heritage buildings are in al-Ifrang, and that most of the distinctive heritage buildings in al-Arab had been replaced with new buildings that are similar to other buildings in Egypt. He felt that al-Arab had become too commercial to be included in the walks they organize. After a few seconds of silence, he added that he still believes that Port Sa'id 'ala Qadimo has to make more efforts to integrate al-Arab in its walks and activities. The first part of Mus'ad's answer raises the question of what is perceived as heritage and what is not, revealing a specific perception of Port Said and what defines it and its heritage. The concept of heritage itself is not neutral, but is constructed through processes of abstraction and fetishization of spaces. Drawing on Marx's (1977) explanation of the fetishization of commodities, Lefebvre (1991) argues that capitalism also fetishizes space. It renders space a mere abstraction, detaching it from the labor force and the social relations that produced it in the first place. Al-Ifrang was built as the European façade of the city, hiding al-Arab as an undesirable part that needed to be concealed. Focusing on al-Ifrang as the real face of Port Said—which needs to be protected and preserved—stems from the same perception. It conceals the spatial and social antagonism between al-Ifrang and al-Arab, favoring the colonial architecture of the former.

The argument here is not about the ethics of focusing on al-Ifrang while neglecting al-Arab. It is more about unpacking the abstractions that control the imagination and the process of reproducing spaces. The act of walking around the city and narrating the history of its places is in itself an act of reproducing space and history and thus cannot be neutral. As Benjamin (1969a) emphasizes, history is not the homogenous and empty time that historicism preaches about. On the contrary, it is a rupture that can disrupt the now-time. Also, space is not neutral; it is produced. Both history and space are loaded with the social relations and antagonisms that produce them. These antagonisms may be concealed through abstraction and fetishization processes. However, this will not make the antagonisms disappear. This is the main argument in Gordillo's (2014) work on rubble and ruins. The former signifies the debris of the past that disrupts the present time, while the latter signifies the rubble after fetishizing it, turning it into something that belongs only to the past, detached from the present time, a mere heritage. The process of turning rubble to ruin is the act of concealing the antagonisms that produced this rubble in the first place. In the case of Port Sa'id 'ala Qadimo, the rubble-to-ruin project is still developing. It is still too early to analyze its approach as merely rendering the city into ruins, especially since slight differences in the group's approach are taking place, as will now be explained.

In January 2016, I participated in a workshop in Port Said about the different approaches to reading and reconstructing history. It was organized by the historian Alia Mossallam, who dedicated part of her PhD dissertation to the subject of Port Said during the Suez Crisis. Mossallam was interested in studying the history of the Nasserist period, relying on oral history and popular songs. Port Sa'id 'ala Qadimo was one of the local partners that helped to organize and host the workshop. One of the sessions was on how to read the history of the city by following its spatial transformations. It was organized and moderated by Yahia Shawkat, an urbanism scholar. He arranged a tour in the city that was totally different from the walks of Port Sa'id 'ala Qadimo, incorporating parts of the city that they had never included. Mus'ad himself acknowledged that he had not visited these places or thought of them as parts of "the identity of Port Said" before the workshop. The tour started from al-Ifrang, cut across al-Arab, al-Manakh, and al-Zuhur, and ended at the shantytown on the shore of Lake al-Manzala. All of these places told fragments of the story of the city, which sounded totally different from the story that al-Ifrang was telling. The workshop affected Mus'ad and Misho, who both attended it.

When I attended the Spring Festival exhibition of Port Sa'id 'ala Qadimo in April 2017, I found that they added a banner of pictures of figures who were members of the resistance during *al-'udwan al thulathi* (the Tripartite Aggression), with short biographies of them. There was another banner with lyrics of *simsimiya* songs and the events about which they were written and sung. Mus'ad also told me that in October 2016, Port Sa'id 'ala Qadimo was part of an event called Mahtat ("stops") that took place in three cities simultaneously, Port Said being one of them. It consisted of outdoor and interactive audio and visual performances in the three cities. Port Sa'id 'ala Qadimo chose a building in al-Arab to be part of the event. The building served as a theater for the audio/visual performance, using lights and music to highlight different parts of the building while a performer narrated the story of the neighborhood. The audience, participating in the show, were pedestrians in the street, residents in their houses, and people in the cafés. Mus'ad said that this was the first time they had organized an activity in al-Arab and that it made them realize that they should do it more often. It is true that the colonial narrative of Port Said still dominates Port Saʻid ʻala Qadimo's work, but some traces of other narratives have started to appear. Still, assembling different narratives and putting them in one place does not mean that the narrative of the city is now more inclusive. What is actually needed is to narrate the story of the city based on the social and spatial antagonisms among its groups and neighborhoods.

There is arguably a link between Port Saʻid ʻala Qadimo, Suhba, and the other *simsimiya* bands that makes their work crucial: their claim to the public spaces of Port Said. Suhba, just like other *simsimiya* bands, performs regularly in public spaces. Suhba started in one of the cafés, then moved to another one. Sawt al-Salam plays in the Saʻd Zaghlul public garden in al-Arab. Al-Tanbura plays in the al-Nigmah café. The Port Saʻid ʻala Qadimo walks are public activities that take place in the streets of the city. The existence of these activities in the public spaces encourages a sense of communal ownership of the spaces of the city. The fact that these public spaces are occupied by cultural and artistic events does not negate the fact that consuming public spaces is one of the ways to define who owns the city and reproduces it. Despite the problematic approach of Port Saʻid ʻala Qadimo in dealing with the concept of "heritage," their walks still contribute to the making of the city by claiming the right to walk and to reuse the old buildings. The very idea of reusing the spaces of the city changes the relationship of the residents with the city, reinforcing a sense of ownership and belonging.

CHAPTER 6

Conclusions and Reflections

*Memories tie us to that place.... It's personal, not interesting to any-
one else, but after all that's what gives a neighborhood its character.*
(de Certeau 1984:108)

In this study, I have attempted to trace the different ways in which the
social of Port Said has been assembled, and the ways in which the spaces
of the city have been produced through the practices of the residents
and the state. I focused on the processes of the making of the people
and the city in specific moments: *al-tahgir* (the forced migration that
followed the outbreak of the 1967 war and continued until 1974); the
declaration of the Free Trade Zone in the mid 1970s; and the Port Said
Stadium Massacre in 2012. However, I did not choose these moments at
the beginning of my fieldwork. They emerged as pivotal moments while
I was conducting my fieldwork. They were pivotal because in each one of
them, different actors emerged, different groups were formed, and spaces
were produced. They were fragments through which the history of Port
Said could be narrated, not as it happened, but as it was experienced.

During *al-tahgir*, the evacuation of Port Said threatened Port Saidians by alienating them from the forms of existence they had previously
used to define their lives, such as residence, work, and socialization. Being
away from the space that allowed these forms of existence—and that was
simultaneously produced through them—generated the process of reimagining Port Said as developed, modernized, and open to the world in
comparison to the host communities, which were rendered as rural, primitive, and parochial. *Simsimiya*, as an actor, played a major role in forging
this imagination about Port Said during *al-tahgir*. The *simsimiya* gatherings were nodes of reproducing the Port Saidians as a group, while they
were away from their city. The migration documents were other actors,

93

which produced *al-muhaggarin* (the evacuees) as legal subjects. Later, these documents were used as proof of Port-Saidness against *al-aghrab*.

The declaration of the FTZ shifted the modality of trading in Port Said, from sea trading to land trading. It allowed new actors such as smugglers, holders of import permits, middlemen, street vendors, and local visitors to emerge, transforming the landscape of the city. The trading hub moved from the al-Ifrang neighborhood to al-Arab. The mobility of the ships, goods, gifts, and foreign visitors was replaced with the confinement of the imported commodities within the borders of the Free Trade Zone. Trading shifted from being a way to communicate with the world to an affair confined to the local. It can be argued that the city was rendered as the symbol of *infitah* (the open door policy), after being the icon of the resistance during the Tripartite Aggression in 1956.

After the decay of the Free Trade Zone, a sense of disorientation haunted both the sea and land traders. The commercial streets in al-Arab became an open-air museum of the devastated lives of the traders. The prison massacre affected the people of the city deeply. It rendered them as "thugs" and "perpetrators," posing the question "What is Port Said beyond the massacre?" The answer came in the form of new practices to reproduce the city in different ways. Through different practices, different fragments of the past are recalled to reinvent the city as the icon of resistance, or a city with unique architecture and a cosmopolitan past, or a city with a distinctive musical heritage. Through the walks of the Port Sa'id 'ala Qadimo (Port Said as It Was) group and the concerts of new *simsimiya* bands in public spaces, a sense of belonging to Port Said was developed, and claims to the spaces of the city were made. However, both forms of practices engage with the past, which is rendered as heritage, in an ambiguous way. On one hand, Port Sa'id 'ala Qadimo and the new *simsimiya* bands fetishize the past of the city, while on the other hand, they use this past to claim the right to the city and its spaces.

The reinvention of Port Said has not stopped. In the past two years, President Sisi announced the beginning of a series of projects in the eastern part of Port Said: a new port, a mega industrial zone, and a new city of 50,000 people. These projects are part of the government plan to "develop the Suez Canal Zone." They raise questions about the effects of these projects on Port Said. Will we see a new wave of migration to Port Said similar to that of the nineteenth century? In what way will these new spaces be ordered? What will the relationship be between the new Port Said and the old one? If Port Said was part of building modern Egypt, what will the role of the new Port Said be? All of these questions may lead to further research projects to understand not only what is happening in Port Said now but also what is happening in Egypt generally.

Through this journey, Port Said was not produced merely by the state or by plans drawn up in the capital. Rather, the networks of actors always went beyond these two influential and hegemonic structures of power. The people of Port Said were always actors themselves, also playing a part in the reinventions of the city. However, there has always been a question of how to theorize concepts such as the state or the capital through a conceptual framework that relies on the Actor Network Theory—a question that was not fully addressed in this research. As a preliminary reflection to open up possibilities for further research, I suggest that, for instance, the state can also be theorized as a group of actors who work together in a specific way in order to sustain the group's domination or to maintain a specific order. We can follow the same paradigm of the Actor Network Theory to understand state formation and transformation as processes involving a group, or even various groups, of actors rather than one solidified entity. What makes this assumption possible is the fact that each time I asked one of my interlocutors about the state and how it was transformed with time, the answer was always vague and unclear. However, as the interview progressed, the same interlocutor was always able to provide specific details about state practices, and their effects on their lives and the city. For instance, the migration documents, the import permits, and the customs officers are all actors that affected the lives of the Port Saidians, and they belong to the realm of the state; they form a diffused network of actors that influence other groups of actors.

What makes any city interesting is the fact that it is the most intimate space in which we practice our existence. The city is what we have, what we produce, and what makes us. In this study, I have attempted to situate this intimacy as the cornerstone of my understanding of how the spaces of the cities are developed, and how lives are produced. It was an attempt to read Port Said from below instead of from above, knowing that it is a messy process of collecting and ordering fragments; yet within the messiness there is also a way to develop alternative knowledge and policies about cities.

References

Abdel Shakur, M. A., S. Mehanna, and N. S. Hopkins. 2005. "War and Forced Migration in Egypt: The Experience of Evacuation from the Suez Canal Cities (1967–1976)," *Arab Studies Quarterly*, 27(3): 21–39. http://www.jstor.org/stable/41858507

Benjamin, Walter. 1969a. "Thesis on the Philosophy of History." In Hannah Arendt, ed. *Illuminations*, 253–264. New York: Harcourt, Brace & World.

Benjamin, Walter. 1969b. "The Storyteller: Reflections on the Works of Nikolai Leskov." In Hannah Arendt, ed. *Illuminations*, 253–264. New York: Harcourt, Brace & World.

Das, Veena. 2007. *Life and Words: Violence and the Descent into the Ordinary*. Berkeley: University of California Press.

De Certeau, Michel. 1984. *The Practice of Everyday Life*. Berkeley: University of California Press.

Elgezy, Ahmed. 2017. *Asma' shawari' Port Sa'id: sira' al-sultah 'ala al-taryikh* [Names of Port Said Streets: The Power Struggle over History]. AlManassa website. https://tinyurl.com/w6m6vq3

Fernea, Robert A., and John G. Kennedy. 1966. "Initial Adaptations to Resettlement: A New Life for Egyptian Nubians," *Current Anthropology*, 7(3): 349–354. http://www.jstor.org/stable/2740060

Frémaux, Céline, and Mercedes Volait. 2009. "Inventing Space in the Age of Empire: Planning Experiments and Achievements along Suez Canal in Egypt (1859–1956)," *Planning Perspectives*, 24(2): 255–262. http://dx.doi.org/10.1080/02665430902734350

Gordillo, Gaston R. 2014. *Rubble: The Afterlife of Destruction*. Durham, NC: Duke University Press.

Harvey, David. 1989. "From Managerialism to Entrepreneurialism: The Transformation in Urban Governance in Late Capitalism," *Geografiska Annaler. Series B, Human Geography*, 71(1): 3–17. http://www.jstor.org/stable/490503

Hassan, Gamal. 2016. *Port Fouad 1973: Waqa'i sanawat al-gamr* [Port Fouad 1973: Chronicles of the Years of Ember]. Cairo: Egyptian Public Authority for Books.

Kalfat, M. F. 2013. *Port Said: Laylah wa subhiya* [Port Said: A Night and a Morning]. https://tinyurl.com/ybctww47

Khalili, Laleh. 2007. "Heroic and Tragic Pasts: Mnemonic Narratives in the Palestinian Refugee Camps," *Critical Sociology*, 33: 731–759. DOI: 10.1163/156916307X211017.

Latour, Bruno. 2005. *Reassembling the Social: An Introduction to the Actor Network Theory*. New York: Oxford University Press.

Lefebvre, Henri. 1991. *Production of Space*. Oxford: Blackwell.

Marx, Karl. 1977 [1867]. *Capital: A Critique of Political Economy*. Vol. 1. New York: Vintage.

Mitchell, Timothy. 1991. *Colonising Egypt*. Berkeley, Los Angeles, and London: University of California Press.

Mohamed Abbas, Mohamed Medhat. 2001. "System of Free Cities and Its Effect on Local Decision Making." Unpublished master's thesis: Suez Canal University.

Mohie, Mostafa, and Waad Ahmed. 2017. "Development 'Alternatives' Raise Fear of Forced Relocation from Maspero Triangle," Mada Masr, 16 March. https://tinyurl.com/ukplg59

Mossallam, Alia. 2012. "*Hikayat sha'b*: Stories of Peoplehood, Nasserism, Popular Politics and Songs in Egypt, 1956–1973." Unpublished doctoral dissertation: London School of Economics and Political Science.

Mubarak, Aly Pasha. 1886–1888. *Al-khitat al-jadidah l-Misr: al-Qahirah wa muduniha wa biladiha al-qadima wa-l-shahira* [New Plans of Egypt: Cairo and Its Old and Famous Cities]. Cairo: Al-Amiriya Press.

Navaro-Yashin, Y. 2012. *The Make-Believe Space: Affective Geography in a Postwar Polity*. Durham, NC: Duke University Press.

Negm, Zain al-ʿAbedin. 1987. *Port Saʿid: nashʾatuha wa tatawuriha* [Port Said: Its Establishment and Development]. Cairo: Egyptian Public Authority for Books.

Saleh, Sayed. 2012. "Qarar al-raʾis bizyadat al-hissah al-ʿistiradiyah yaftah abwab al-amal" [The President's Decision to Increase the Importing Quota Opens a Door for Hope]. *Al-Ahram*, 18 July. http://www.ahram.org.eg/archive/Investigations/News/161042.aspx

Scott, James C. 1998. *Seeing Like a State: How Certain Schemes to Improve the Human Condition Have Failed*. London and New Haven: Yale University Press.

Simone, AbdouMaliq. 2004. "People as Infrastructure: Intersecting Fragments in Johannesburg," *Public Culture*, 16(3): 407–429.

Suez Canal Authority. 1958. *Suez Canal Report*. Ismailiya: Suez Canal Authority Press.

Suez Canal Authority. 1964. *Suez Canal Report*. Ismailiya: Suez Canal Authority Press.

About the Author

Mostafa Mohie is a journalist who works for the Mada Masr website in Egypt. He participated as a researcher in two documentary films about the Alexandrian trade unionist Fathallah Mahrous and the Ezbet Khairallah neighborhood in Cairo. He holds an MA in cultural anthropology from the American University in Cairo. This manuscript is based on his MA thesis.

CAIRO PAPERS IN SOCIAL SCIENCE

Volume Six

1 *The Political Economy of Revolutionary Iran*, Mihssen Kadhim
2 *Urban Research Strategies in Egypt*, Richard A. Lobban, ed.
3 *Non-alignment in a Changing World*, Mohammed el-Sayed Selim, ed.
4 *The Nationalization of Arabic and Islamic Education in Egypt: Dar al-Alum and al-Azhar*, Lois A. Aroian

Volume Seven

1 *Social Security and the Family in Egypt*, Helmi Tadros
2 *Basic Needs, Inflation and the Poor of Egypt*, Myrette el-Sokkary
3 *The Impact of Development Assistance on Egypt*, Earl L. Sullivan, ed.
4 *Irrigation and Society in Rural Egypt*, Sohair Mehanna, Richard Huntington, and Rachad Antonius

Volume Eight

1, 2 *Analytic Index of Survey Research in Egypt*, Madiha el-Safty, Monte Palmer, and Mark Kennedy

Volume Nine

1 *Philosophy, Ethics and Virtuous Rule*, Charles E. Butterworth
2 *The 'Jihad': An Islamic Alternative in Egypt*, Nemat Guenena
3 *The Institutionalization of Palestinian Identity in Egypt*, Maha A. Dajani
4 *Social Identity and Class in a Cairo Neighborhood*, Nadia A. Taher

Volume Ten

1 *Al-Sanhuri and Islamic Law*, Enid Hill
2 *Gone for Good*, Ralph Sell
3 *The Changing Image of Women in Rural Egypt*, Mona Abaza
4 *Informal Communities in Cairo: the Basis of a Typology*, Linda Oldham, Haguer el Hadidi, and Hussein Tamaa

Volume Eleven

1 *Participation and Community in Egyptian New Lands: The Case of South Tahrir*, Nicholas Hopkins et al.
2 *Palestinian Universities under Occupation*, Antony T. Sullivan
3 *Legislating Infitah: Investment, Foreign Trade and Currency Laws*, Khaled M. Fahmy
4 *Social History of an Agrarian Reform Community in Egypt*, Reem Saad

Volume Twelve

1 *Cairo's Leap Forward: People, Households, and Dwelling Space*, Fredric Shorter
2 *Women, Water, and Sanitation: Household Water Use in Two Egyptian Villages*, Samiha el-Katsha et al.
3 *Palestinian Labor in a Dependent Economy: Women Workers in the West Bank Clothing Industry*, Randa Siniora
4 *The Oil Question in Egyptian-Israeli Relations, 1967–1979: A Study in International Law and Resource Politics*, Karim Wissa

Volume Thirteen

1 *Squatter Markets in Cairo*, Helmi R. Tadros, Mohamed Feteeha, and Allen Hibbard
2 *The Sub-culture of Hashish Users in Egypt: A Descriptive Analytic Study*, Nashaat Hassan Hussein
3 *Social Background and Bureaucratic Behavior in Egypt*, Earl L. Sullivan, el Sayed Yassin, Ali Leila, and Monte Palmer
4 *Privatization: The Egyptian Debate*, Mostafa Kamel el-Sayyid

Volume Fourteen

1 *Perspectives on the Gulf Crisis*, Dan Tschirgi and Bassam Tibi
2 *Experience and Expression: Life among Bedouin Women in South Sinai*, Deborah Wickering
3 *Impact of Temporary International Migration on Rural Egypt*, Atef Hanna Nada
4 *Informal Sector in Egypt*, Nicholas S. Hopkins, ed.

Volume Fifteen

1 *Scenes of Schooling: Inside a Girls' School in Cairo*, Linda Herrera
2 *Urban Refugees: Ethiopians and Eritreans in Cairo*, Dereck Cooper
3 *Investors and Workers in the Western Desert of Egypt: An Exploratory Survey*, Naeim Sherbiny, Donald Cole, and Nadia Makary
4 *Environmental Challenges in Egypt and the World*, Nicholas S. Hopkins, ed.

Volume Sixteen

1 *The Socialist Labor Party: A Case Study of a Contemporary Egyptian Opposition Party*, Hanaa Fikry Singer
2 *The Empowerment of Women: Water and Sanitation Initiatives in Rural Egypt*, Samiha el Katsha and Susan Watts
3 *The Economics and Politics of Structural Adjustment in Egypt: Third Annual Symposium*

4   *Experiments in Community Development in a Zabbaleen Settlement*, Marie
     Assaad and Nadra Garas

Volume Seventeen

1   *Democratization in Rural Egypt: A Study of the Village Local Popular
     Council*, Hanan Hamdy Radwan
2   *Farmers and Merchants: Background for Structural Adjustment in Egypt*,
     Sohair Mehanna, Nicholas S. Hopkins, and Bahgat Abdelmaksoud
3   *Human Rights: Egypt and the Arab World, Fourth Annual Symposium*
4   *Environmental Threats in Egypt: Perceptions and Actions*, Salwa S. Gomaa, ed.

Volume Eighteen

1   *Social Policy in the Arab World*, Jacqueline Ismael and Tareq Y. Ismael
2   *Workers, Trade Union and the State in Egypt: 1984–1989*, Omar el-Shafie
3   *The Development of Social Science in Egypt: Economics, History and
     Sociology; Fifth Annual Symposium*
4   *Structural Adjustment, Stabilization Policies and the Poor in Egypt*, Karima
     Korayem

Volume Nineteen

1   *Nilopolitics: A Hydrological Regime, 1870–1990*, Mohamed Hatem el-Atawy
2   *Images of the Other: Europe and the Muslim World before 1700*, David R.
     Blanks et al.
3   *Grass Roots Participation in the Development of Egypt*, Saad Eddin
     Ibrahim et al.
4   *The Zabbalin Community of Muqattam*, Elena Volpi and Doaa Abdel Motaal

Volume Twenty

1   *Class, Family, and Power in an Egyptian Village*, Samer el-Karanshawy
2   *The Middle East and Development in a Changing World*, Donald Heisel, ed.
3   *Arab Regional Women's Studies Workshop*, Cynthia Nelson and Soraya
     Altorki, eds.
4   *"Just a Gaze": Female Clientele of Diet Clinics in Cairo: An Ethnomedical
     Study*, Iman Farid Bassyouny

Volume Twenty-one

1   *Turkish Foreign Policy during the Gulf War of 1990–1991*, Mostafa Aydin
2   *State and Industrial Capitalism in Egypt*, Samer Soliman
3   *Twenty Years of Development in Egypt (1977–1997): Part I*, Mark C. Kennedy
4   *Twenty Years of Development in Egypt (1977–1997): Part II*, Mark C. Kennedy

Volume Twenty-two

1 *Poverty and Poverty Alleviation Strategies in Egypt*, Ragui Assaad and Malak Rouchdy

2 *Between Field and Text: Emerging Voices in Egyptian Social Science*, Seteney Shami and Linda Hererra, eds.

3 *Masters of the Trade: Crafts and Craftspeople in Cairo, 1750–1850*, Pascale Ghazaleh

4 *Discourses in Contemporary Egypt: Politics and Social Issues*, Enid Hill, ed.

Volume Twenty-three

1 *Fiscal Policy Measures in Egypt: Public Debt and Food Subsidy*, Gouda Abdel-Khalek and Karima Korayem

2 *New Frontiers in the Social History of the Middle East*, Enid Hill, ed.

3 *Egyptian Encounters*, Jason Thompson, ed.

4 *Women's Perception of Environmental Change in Egypt*, Eman el Ramly

Volume Twenty-four

1, 2 *The New Arab Family*, Nicholas S. Hopkins, ed.

3 *An Investigation of the Phenomenon of Polygyny in Rural Egypt*, Laila S. Shahd

4 *The Terms of Empowerment: Islamic Women Activists in Egypt*, Sherine Hafez

Volume Twenty-five

1, 2 *Elections in the Middle East: What Do They Mean?* Iman A. Hamdy, ed.

3 *Employment Crisis of Female Graduates in Egypt: An Ethnographic Account*, Ghada F. Barsoum

4 *Palestinian and Israeli Nationalism: Identity Politics and Education in Jerusalem*, Evan S. Weiss

Volume Twenty-six

1 *Culture and Natural Environment: Ancient and Modern Middle Eastern Texts*, Sharif S. Elmusa, ed.

2 *Street Children in Egypt: Group Dynamics and Subcultural Constituents*, Nashaat Hussein

3 *IMF–Egyptian Debt Negotiations*, Bessma Momani

4 *Forced Migrants and Host Societies in Egypt and Sudan*, Fabienne Le Houérou

Volume Twenty-seven

1, 2 *Cultural Dynamics in Contemporary Egypt*, Maha Abdelrahman, Iman A. Hamdy, Malak Rouchdy, and Reem Saad, eds.

3   *The Role of Local Councils in Empowerment and Poverty Reduction*, Solava
     Ibrahim
4   *Beach Politics: Gender and Sexuality in Dahab*, Mustafa Abdalla

Volume Twenty-eight
1   *Creating Families across Boundaries: A Case Study of Romanian/Egyptian
     Mixed Marriages*, Ana Vinea
2, 3 *Pioneering Feminist Anthropology in Egypt: Selected Writings from Cynthia
     Nelson*, Martina Rieker, ed.
4   *Roses in Salty Soil: Women and Depression in Egypt Today*, Dalia A. Mostafa

Volume Twenty-nine
1   *Crossing Borders, Shifting Boundaries: Palestinian Dilemmas*, Sari Hanafi,
     ed.
2, 3 *Political and Social Protest in Egypt*, Nicholas S. Hopkins, ed.
4   *The Experience of Protest: Masculinity and Agency among Sudanese Refugees
     in Cairo*, Martin T. Rowe

Volume Thirty
1   *Child Protection Policies in Egypt: A Rights-Based Approach*, Adel Azer,
     Sohair Mehanna, Mulki Al-Sharmani, and Essam Ali
2   *"The Farthest Place": Social Boundaries in an Egyptian Desert Community*,
     Joseph Viscomi
3   *The New York Egyptians: Voyages and Dreams*, Yasmine M. Ahmed
4   *The Burden of Resources: Oil and Water in the Gulf and the Nile Basin*, Sharif
     S. Elmusa, ed.

Volume Thirty-one
1   *Humanist Perspectives on Sacred Space*, David Blanks, Bradley S. Clough,
     eds.
2   *Law as a Tool for Empowering Women within Marital Relations: A Case
     Study of Paternity Lawsuits in Egypt*, Hind Ahmed Zaki
3, 4 *Visual Productions of Knowledge: Toward a Different Middle East*, Hanan
     Sabea, Mark R. Westmoreland, eds.

Volume Thirty-two
1   *Planning Egypt's New Settlements: The Politics of Spatial Inequities*, Dalia
     Wahdan
2   *Agrarian Transformation in the Arab World: Persistent and Emerging
     Challenges*, Habib Ayeb and Reem Saad